Bonhoeffer's Ethic of Discipleship

What prepares men for totalitarian domination in the non-totalitarian world is the fact that loneliness, once a borderline experience usually suffered in certain marginal social conditions like old age, has become an everyday experience of the evergrowing masses of our century. . . .

But there remains also the truth that every end in history necessarily contains a new beginning; this beginning is the promise, the only "message" which the end can ever produce. Beginning, before it becomes a historical event, is the supreme capacity of man; politically, it is identical with man's freedom. Initium ut esset homo creatus est— *"that a beginning be made man was created," said Augustine. This beginning is guaranteed by each new birth; it is indeed every man.*

—Hannah Arendt, *The Origins of Totalitarianism*

If anyone thinks of God as anything other than life itself, he has an absurd idea of God.

—Augustine

Bonhoeffer's Ethic of Discipleship

A Study in Social Psychology, Political Thought, and Religion

Kenneth Earl Morris

THE PENNSYLVANIA STATE UNIVERSITY PRESS
University Park and London

Library of Congress Cataloging-in-Publication Data

Morris, Kenneth Earl, 1955–
Bonhoeffer's ethic of discipleship.

Includes bibliography and index.
1. Bonhoeffer, Dietrich, 1906–1945—Contributions in
concept of discipleship.   2. Christian life—History—
20th century.   3. Christian ethics—History—20th
century.   I. Title.
BV4490.M66   1986   241'.092'4   85–31949
ISBN 0–271–00428–2

Contents

Preface

The idea for a study of Dietrich Bonhoeffer occurred to me while I was searching for a topic through which to explore a threefold interest in psychological development, political thought, and religion. Bonhoeffer, I remembered, was one of only a handful of clergymen who had become involved in the German Resistance to the point of conspiracy to assassinate Hitler. He was also a theological thinker of considerable reputation. His posthumous *Letters and Papers from Prison* virtually defined the theological agenda during the 1950s and 1960s, and his 1937 book *The Cost of Discipleship* was still cropping up in discussions of the relationship between Christian faith and political action. In the combined legacy of this theologian and political actor, I reasoned, was

a subject of considerable intrigue for those of us concerned with
the relationship between faith and politics in the modern world.
Even the historical timing was right: predating the current interest
in political or liberation theology, Bonhoeffer nevertheless lived
and acted in the epoch that inaugurated our distinctly modern—
or postmodern—age, the years of World War II.

What remained for me to determine was to what extent Bonhoeffer might be subjected to a psychological interpretation. Now,
in principle, anyone can be the subject of psychological interpretation, but, in fact, such a test is not equally revealing of everyone.
The reason is that a psychological context is really only one of
many contexts that may influence a person's thought or action.
Many people—probably most throughout history—after all, probably have acted or thought more in a social or cultural context
than a psychological one. Indeed, it requires almost a special self-
absorption (that is in itself characteristically modern) to elevate
one's psychology to the status of a central context out of which
thought and action spring. Therefore, it remained for me to determine to what extent Bonhoeffer might be fruitfully interpreted in
a psychological context.

As it happened, Bonhoeffer proved to be an ideal candidate
for psychological interpretation, as almost all Bonhoeffer scholars
were agreed that it was the psychological context of his family,
more so than the religious context of his church or the political
context of his country, that provided the best setting for interpreting his thought and action. Also, although there is never
"enough" material, it turned out that plenty of primary and secondary sources spoke to his psychological development within
the family, so a study of the sort I envisioned was possible—even
if it could never be exhaustive.

Only after digging into Bonhoeffer's story did I reach two initial
conclusions that helped me clarify the focus of the study. One
was that if my interest was in the relationships among psychology,

religion, and politics, my study ought to focus primarily upon Bonhoeffer's theology of discipleship rather than upon either his earlier and less well-known thought or his later and probably better-known *Letters and Papers from Prison*. This focus became necessary because, as it turned out, it was discipleship that dominated Bonhoeffer's thought between 1932 and at least 1939, though perhaps until the early 1940s—the period that paralleled the rise of Nazism in Germany and so the time of Bonhoeffer's political action. I came then to understand Bonhoeffer's earlier thought as a kind of prelude to discipleship and his later writings as actually something quite different: almost a transcending of discipleship. Of course, I acknowledge the theological importance of especially his late thought as embodied in *Letters and Papers from Prison*, and I also find the dramatic change in his thought at this stage psychologically revealing, but so far as Bonhoeffer's significance as a political actor is concerned his late thought is tangential. This much can be realized simply by listening to current discussions of Christian political responsibility that often employ the catchword "discipleship" but almost never the catchphrase of *Letters and Papers from Prison*, "religionless Christianity." The latter inspires reflection; the former, action.

Related to this focusing of the study on discipleship was my initial awareness that in studying discipleship I was not studying a theology so much as I was an ethic. To be sure, there is a theology of discipleship contained in the pages of *The Cost of Discipleship* that commentators can and do interpret. But that theology, I soon realized, was not really my interest. Instead, I was interested in discipleship more in the way I think Bonhoeffer was interested in it, more in the way later Christians are interested in it: as a way of life, an ethic, an "experiment with truth." Anyone familiar with Bonhoeffer's life, I think, will understand what I mean by this. For the decade or so that Bonhoeffer was consumed with a passion for discipleship, that passion was primarily praxic rather than theological. He wanted, I believe, to learn how to *live* a Christian life, not only how to think about one. Because of his orientation, therefore, I consider discipleship to be a practical Christian ethic over and above a theological statement and so I interpret it as such. Hence my lines of interpretation are anchored in the sociological and psychological traditions of the study of Christian ethics rather than in the theological traditions; my object of inquiry is defined from the outset as a problem of praxis, not of thought.

The other conclusion I reached early that helped to clarify the focus of the study was that my psychological orientation was neither optional nor accidental; rather, the very possibility of a psychological interpretation was itself part of the problem to be investigated—and part of the conclusion that needed to be reached. What I slowly began to realize is that the hallmark of the contemporary age is not authoritarianism but the eclipse of authority and its replacement by an ethic of authenticity. Increasingly we define our existence in terms of the structures within us rather than the structures outside us. It followed that the possibility of a psychological interpretation of a religious thinker and political actor in modern times was not so much an option as it was a necessity: the only kind of person who could speak to modern times is one who speaks in a language of authenticity rather than authority, or in terms of psychology as well as politics or religion. So it also followed that the appropriateness of a psychological interpretation of Bonhoeffer was surely no accident, but was rather an indication of his stature as a thoroughly modern person. Thus I concluded that a psychological interpretation was not only one among many possible interpretive strategies but also was perhaps the central interpretive strategy for contemporary discourse. With this in mind I have endeavored to work into the study the motif of psychology not only as a method or perspective but also as a partner in theological dialogue and political discussion. At the same time, however, I have striven to avoid creating the impression that psychology replaces theology or politics, for ultimately I believe that the psychological approach is but a historically necessary one given the present state of our society and that, ideally, it should be used only to create new bonds of sociality—of authority—and not as an end in itself.

This study was long in the making, and there are many people I need to thank for helping me to conceive and complete it. At its early stage, discussions with Barbara Terry, mostly about social thought and feminism, and Dick Morley, mostly about family dynamics, helped me to formulate the undertaking. Professors John Haag and Eugene Miller at the University of Georgia also helped me in this stage by allowing me to audit their courses in fascism and political philosophy, respectively. Later Professor Lindsey Rogers provided a similar service by allowing me to audit his course in German. Clifford Green of the International Bonhoeffer Society for Archive and Research, English Language Section, aided my initial research by responding thoughtfully to some of my queries. Philip Abbott, Robert Ayers, Jack Balswick, Gene Brody, Donald Capps, Roger Johnson, Robin Lovin, George Moraitis, Barry Schwartz, and Raymond Yang all read and commented on earlier drafts of the manuscript. Schwartz and Yang deserve special thanks, as each of them read three different versions—and encouraged me to keep rewriting until I had it right. Their role was taken over by John Pickering of the Pennsylvania State University Press, who mediated between my various revisions and critiques of several readers engaged by the Press. Without his assistance and encouragement, this study would never have grown into the book it has become. Despite the influence of all these people on this book, however, I alone must remain responsible for its shortcomings.

I

Introduction: The Burden
of Discipleship

With the posthumous publication of his *Letters and Papers from Prison*, Dietrich Bonhoeffer has become widely known as a harbinger for a novel and enigmatic Christianity that he called "religionless Christianity" for a "world come of age."[1] Written during his confinement in a Nazi prison cell in the two years prior to his execution in 1945, these letters and papers shocked the theological world. Shocking, first of all, was the identity of their author: a German pastor and theologian whose faith apparently had led him to join the resistance movement and conspire to overthrow the Reich and assassinate Hitler. But shocking too was the content of these letters and papers. Although still committed to thinking "theologically," as he put it, Bonhoeffer in 1944 was expressing odd-sounding ideas about the world having outgrown its need for "religious tutelage" and this being a good thing that might pave the way for genuine faith. These ideas both fitted and did not fit with the legacy of a man whose commitment to the church had led him through an instrumental role in the German church struggle to a position as political conspirator and beyond. The call sounded in *Letters and Papers from Prison* was one of a Christian who had lived and acted in one of history's most perilous and paradoxical times and had come out with a different kind of faith— yet still a faith. The call is the amazing one that religious faith must now be grounded in strength and not weakness, that faith itself must be severed from religious trappings, that "before God and with God we live without God."[2]

What sense can be made of so strange and paradoxical a call? It is not surprising that many interpreters, especially at first, simply dismissed it as "prison psychosis."[3] Neither is it much more surprising that other interpreters have read into Bonhoeffer's words pretty much anything they liked so long as it celebrated secularity.[4] And in a domain open to such extreme interpretations either way, it is probably not surprising that most responsible Bonhoeffer scholars today attempt to put these enigmatic utterances in the more subdued biographical context in which they were actually embedded. Specifically, most of what is really radical in Bonhoeffer's writings appears only in fragments of letters and notes written during the last year of his life, and most interpreters can quite reasonably afford to minimize these later writings' significance by tackling the weightier bulk of Bonhoeffer's thought and by observing that the imprisoned Bonhoeffer was not allowed to live and write the work he was contemplating, which would have clarified these last strange-sounding remarks.

The present book defers to this prevailing mood of Bonhoeffer scholarship by de-emphasizing these final and fragmented comments of Bonhoeffer in favor of a more detailed scrutiny of certain aspects of his earlier thought: what I will call the ethic of discipleship. However, there is an important exception to this omission: irrespective of the specific interpretation of the call for a "religionless Christianity," I wish to set up the fact of this call as a liberating episode in Bonhoeffer's biography. That is, whatever the specific interpretation given it, it is clear that the call for "religionless Christianity" represents a personal and intellectual triumph for Bonhoeffer, as it also has for most of the rest of the world (the evidence for which is the status of *Letters and Papers from Prison* as a "religious classic" contrary to the expectations of either author or compiler[5]).

That this was, as a matter of fact, also Bonhoeffer's view, is suggested in several ways. For one, as Ott observes,[6] it was upon the following passage in Jeremiah that Bonhoeffer meditated time and again while in prison:

> Behold what I have built I am breaking down, and what I have planted I am plucking up, even this whole land. And do you seek great things for yourself? Seek them not. For behold I am bringing evil upon all flesh, says the Lord; but I will give you your life as a prize of war in all places to which you may go.

And it was the phrase "I will give you your life as a prize of war" that kept recurring in his mind and prose. That he was granted this "prize"—at least briefly—is suggested by his dramatic change from self-absorption and thoughts of suicide during his first year of imprisonment to cheerfulness, helpfulness, and productive theological work in his second year. As he himself put it in April of 1944—twelve months after the beginning of his confinement and in the same month that he wrote the famous letter of 30 April 1944, in which he inaugurates his program of "religionless Christianity"—"If I were to end my life here in these conditions, that would have a meaning that I think I could understand; on the other hand, everything might be a thorough preparation for a new start and a new task when peace comes."[7] Further (and important to the present thesis about the centrality of discipleship to Bonhoeffer's life through his period of political resistance), it was not until July 1944 that he partially dissociated himself from his *Cost of Discipleship*,[8] claiming that it represents the "end" of a path and contains certain "dangers."[9] Finally, there is the most obvious clue of all: that the term he chose to designate the world that had become religionless, *Mündigkeit* in German and translated into English as "coming of age," itself suggests liberation. Literally, it refers to the age of majority, or the age that a child becomes legally an adult. The metaphor that Bonhoeffer selects to characterize the world that is to receive his radically new theology, then, is a metaphor of personal liberation.

For these reasons I consider it justifiable to assume that this final phase of Bonhoeffer's life and thought represents an achievement of liberation. It will be the thrust of this study to show the personal, psychological dimension of this liberation, though it must always be borne in mind in contrast to much of the prevailing tenor in the psychology of religion that, for Bonhoeffer, if this liberation was from dependency on religion, it was nevertheless liberation for faith.

Discipleship: The Intrigue of Bonhoeffer

Had *Letters and Papers from Prison* never been published and the world remained ignorant of Bonhoeffer's final theological reflections, he still would have gone down in history as a member of a special class of historical exemplars. This class of exemplars— to which I can think of only one other person as truly belonging:

Simone Weil—owe their intrigue to a unique and paradoxical position in an equally unique and paradoxical time. The time, of course, is of crucial significance. It was Europe in the 1930s and early 1940s—that is, a Europe which at the height of her intellectual, economic, and cultural flowering became the first civilization in the history of the earth to proceed along the political path we now know as totalitarianism. The paradox of this time is that at its zenith this civilization showed itself capable of nearly complete self-destruction. Thrust most forcefully on the first generation of Westerners in the twentieth century, the burden of this paradox is now carried in the cultural identity of the west itself. The political symbol of this paradox is the death camps, a symbol of total domination, paralleling the potential for global destruction, which finds its own symbol in the mushroom cloud. And there is no escaping the past: so long as our civilization remains, it will be to this epoch in the history of the west that moderns will trace their fundamental doubt in and fragmented allegiance to their civilization.

It was into the first generation to face this crisis of the west that Bonhoeffer was born, a German, in 1906. He was twenty-seven years old when he saw Hitler become chancellor of Germany, and thirty-nine when, in Hitler's final frantic purge, he was executed for conspiracy against the Reich. And this is the first thread that will weave itself into the account of Bonhoeffer's intrigue: that he opposed Nazism from its inception, critiquing the leadership principle in public lectures as early as February 1933,[10] and that in the 1940s he became involved in the political resistance itself, plotting the assassination of Hitler and the overthrow of the Reich in the conspiracy that, although he was imprisoned by the time, eventuated in the plot of 20 July 1944. Among the members of the German Resistance, Bonhoeffer was unique in his vocation. A theologian and Lutheran minister, he was one of only four Protestant pastors who took their opposition to National

Socialism the final step into violent revolt.[11] To be sure, for more than half a decade prior to entering the political resistance itself, Bonhoeffer was an active and ardent spokesperson for the Confessing Church, the Christians who dissociated themselves from the nazification of the churches in the Barmen Declaration of 1934. In his native Germany, in England, and in the ecumenical circles to which he belonged and was committed, Bonhoeffer was one of the most vocal opponents of National Socialism to be found in the church at the time. Yet it was when this opposition was pushed to extreme form in political resistance itself that Bonhoeffer's story becomes paradoxical. For at the same time that he remained committed to the Prince of Peace—and indeed, even bordered on pacifism in his own thought—he nevertheless took up the sword of political rebellion.

This combination of religious vocation and political action would not be paradoxical if Bonhoeffer had developed in his writings a theology of the sort that today might be called a "political theology" or even a "liberation theology." But such is not the case. His writings reveal him to be oriented almost exclusively toward a personal religious search, essentially apolitical or, where political, staunchly traditional and even authoritarian in its orientation. Indeed, the book that takes center stage in my study because it was his major work in the 1930s, *The Cost of Discipleship* (originally published in 1937), was so traditional in its Lutheran teaching on the duty of Christians to obey governmental authorities that, years later, Bonhoeffer referred his Nazi accusers to it as part of his defense against the charge of treason.[12] Nowhere, not even in his later works, does Bonhoeffer's thought present a fully developed, novel political theology. Instead, his writings are dominated by theological and, mostly, practical concerns of the Christian life. The essential paradox of Bonhoeffer's legacy is represented in just this fact: that a leader in the Christian resistance to National Socialism and one of only a handful of pastors to become involved in the conspiracy to assassinate Hitler and overthrow the Reich, was also a conservative, authoritarian, almost pacifistic Lutheran minister. Put another way, the paradox of Bonhoeffer is that he became the church's first "guilty martyr."[13] And, in terms of his enduring cultural significance, the paradox is that a personal quest for religious truth could have such explosive consequences in the political arena.

It is the story of Bonhoeffer during the decade 1933 to 1943, then, that holds the interest of moderns quite apart from *Letters and Papers from Prison*. The decade encapsulates a paradox of the relationship between the religious and the political, and crystallizing this paradox is Bonhoeffer's major work of the decade, *The Cost of Discipleship*, produced at mid-decade. As will be shown shortly, Bonhoeffer began to develop the arguments of *The Cost of Discipleship* in 1932, and their development represents a radical departure from his earlier, more ponderous and turgid theological treatises[14] insofar as discipleship was conceived from its inception to be a more practical study. Indeed, whereas Bonhoeffer wrote his earlier works in months and wrote *The Cost of Discipleship*'s companion piece, *Life Together* (published in 1938), in an even shorter period, *The Cost of Discipleship* took five long years to prepare—a sluggishness for which he received some good-natured kidding from his students. It took so long because it represented for Bonhoeffer more than a theological tract; more than anything, it constituted for him a way of life, an "experiment with truth" for which practical implementation was more important than theological argument. In practice, the theology of discipleship began to emerge as Bonhoeffer took upon himself the task of daily personal meditation on the Sermon on the Mount, for which *The Cost of Discipleship* is most literally a commentary. Another element is more literally portrayed in *Life Together* but was also crucial to the experiment with discipleship: communal Christian living. As a practical ethic for the Christian life, discipleship above all demanded implementation in a Christian community. And in 1935 Bonhoeffer was given the opportunity to practice discipleship in such a community when he received the call from the Confessing Church to head one of its illegal preachers' seminaries, soon to be located at Finkenwalde. At the time Bonhoeffer, disgusted with the nazification of the churches, had taken up pastorates in London and was making plans to study with Gandhi. But when the opportunity arose for him to establish a Christian community in Germany, he jumped at the chance. At Finkenwalde he astonished many by instituting the practice of personal confession and communal living, and it was there that through lectures and practice the ethic of discipleship was forged in Christian community. The seminary was closed by the police in September 1937, and in November of that year *The Cost of Discipleship* was finally published.

The centrality of the theology and practice of discipleship to the story of Bonhoeffer's resistance to the Third Reich cannot be missed. This must be asserted against those who, on the basis of Bonhoeffer's 1944 remark about *The Cost of Discipleship* being the "end" of a path as well as theological and biographical interpretation generally, argue that there is a fairly radical break between the Bonhoeffer of discipleship and the Bonhoeffer of political resistance. My assertion is based upon a number of points of fact and interpretation which may be briefly listed here. First is the proximity of discipleship to resistance in Bonhoeffer's life. Between the publication of *The Cost of Discipleship* and Bonhoeffer's first contacts with the political conspiracy was a span of only two or three months; between its publication and his conscious commitment to political resistance, I think, was only a year and a half. Now, it is true that Bonhoeffer during his clandestine political activities did work on another book that might possibly be a more accurate record of his thought while he was engaged in resistance activities. But this other work, posthumously published as *Ethics*,[15] was never completed by Bonhoeffer and consists only of four different drafts of the book he was trying to write. His failure at writing a book on ethics suggests that during its writing he had not departed significantly from *The Cost of Discipleship*, even though it does suggest his attempt to go beyond it. Moreover, it is difficult to see how *Ethics* differs significantly from *The Cost of Discipleship*; rather, it seems to me more to embellish it. Thus, in conformity with the prevailing view among Bonhoeffer scholars, I consider *Ethics* to be a transitional work, informative primarily for the light it sheds on what came before and after it.

But the centrality of discipleship to Bonhoeffer's life and thought between 1933 and 1943 is suggested from another quarter: Bonhoeffer himself. On one hand, there are passages in *The Cost of Discipleship* that, at least in retrospect, give reason to suspect its political implications. In an often-quoted passage, for example, Bonhoeffer writes: "When Christ calls a man, he bids him to come and die. It may be a death like that of the first disciples who had to leave home and work to follow him, or it may be a death like Luther's, who had to leave the monastery and go out into the world."[16] From historical hindsight, this passage appears as an ominous premonition of Bonhoeffer's own death as a disciple who followed Christ "out into the world," and another example of such a premonition will be given below. Another passage, this time from a 1935 letter that Bonhoeffer wrote to his brother Karl-Friedrich, shows him commenting on the implications of the ethic of discipleship that he was developing: "I know that inwardly I shall be really clear and honest with myself only when I have begun to take seriously the Sermon on the Mount. That is the only source of power capable of blowing up the whole phantas-magoria once and for all. . . . "[17] By "phantasmagoria," the translator adds, Bonhoeffer meant "Hitler and his rule." The Sermon on the Mount, on the other hand, was the biblical basis for the theology and practice of discipleship that the young pastor was developing in 1935. Thus we see that Bonhoeffer—if he could also write with sufficient Lutheran conservatism to use *The Cost of Discipleship* as part of his defense years later—sensed the political implications of discipleship, even if he did not articulate them. To be sure, I am not asserting that in 1935 or even 1937 Bonhoeffer anticipated a role in the political resistance. The political events overtook him with the same frightful speed that they did everyone in the 1930s. What is being asserted here is that at some almost prerational level of awareness, Bonhoeffer in 1935—even in 1932— anticipated a political role for himself. This awareness, moreover, is lodged in his ethic of discipleship, and it is the task of this study to dislodge and articulate it.

A final bit of evidence for the centrality of discipleship to the story told here is a difficult one to weigh but is important nonetheless. This is the testimony of the Christian community. We are led to believe that in Bonhoeffer's lifetime and in his native country *The Cost of Discipleship* gained some popularity. It was not as widely read as *Life Together*, which reportedly was his most popular book, but it was certainly better known than his earlier theological books. It is said that during one of his stays in a Benedictine monastery in Ettal, where he was allowed to stay periodically in the early 1940s and where he worked on his *Ethics*, he overheard some of the monks reading aloud from *The Cost of Discipleship*, much to his surprise. But what was true then is more true today. Any reasonably well-stocked bookstore carries copies of *The Cost of Discipleship* in inexpensive paperback editions, and it is still not uncommon to find church youth groups or seminarians studying it. Indeed, discipleship today has become almost synonymous with Christian social responsibility, most often associated with the Christian Left. What influence Bonhoeffer's book on discipleship has had on this trend is difficult to tell, but it surely has influenced the countless discipleship workshops and seminars that have sprung up around the globe in recent years. The vanguard for the contemporary American Evangelical Left, the Washington-based Sojourners, has included *The Cost of Discipleship* on its list of recommended readings. The church today feels that Bonhoeffer's *Cost of Discipleship* has something crucial to say about Christian political action, even though, as has been seen, the nature of this message remains curiously oblique.

Again, the challenge of this study is to explicate this message, at least in the context of Bonhoeffer's times. That it may have continuing relevance today adds to the excitement.

The Theoretical Axis:
Authority versus Authenticity

The intrigue of Bonhoeffer in the decade before his imprisonment centers on the paradox that at the same time when he was absorbed by a personal, religious search, epitomized by *The Cost of Discipleship*, he was also an ardent opponent of National Socialism. In order to grasp this paradox, we must place the historical facts in the theoretical context of the relationship between authority and authenticity. The common roots of the two terms suggest their etymological and perhaps existential affinity, even though on the level of social practice they are diametrically opposed. Both terms embrace the notion of the inevitability and even desirability of power inequalities, and the requirement that such inequalities be legitimated by means of a philosophy of justice. Where the meanings of the terms diverge is in the arenas to which they are applied. Authority denotes the legitimation of power inequalities in the domain of social and political practice; that is, among persons and groups. Authenticity, on the other hand, suggests an inner regulation of the respective power differences within the soul. And, whereas authority creates the moral mosaic that constitutes a just society even in the face of inequality, authenticity suggests a harmony of the soul wherein the different appetites and desires are ordered internally so as to make a just person.

The relationship between authority and authenticity has been debated since the time of the Greeks. Plato holds that the two are related by means of analogy, and Socrates suggests that analogy in the opening arguments of the *Republic*. In contrast, the arguments Aristotle develops in the *Politics* and elsewhere advance the view that authority and authenticity are fundamentally opposed insofar as a teleological difference exists between political and personal life. In recent years various theorists have revived these debates, though it is Berman who suggests the contemporary relationship between authority and authenticity that is central to the present discussion. He observes that "in a closed, static society governed by fixed norms and traditions which are accepted by all its members, authenticity has no place in the vocabulary of human ideals."[18] In other words, where authority holds firm and is indeed perceived to be legitimate by the members of society, there is little impetus for the quest for authenticity. So far as human ideals are concerned, authority and authenticity are inversely related. But then Berman adds the additional proposition, culled primarily from Montesquieu and Rousseau, that in modern times the quest for authenticity has itself developed a political dimension—"the politics of authenticity" as he puts it. We think here immediately, as does Berman, of such existentialists as Jean-Paul Sartre and Martin Heidegger. And here we find the first suggestive theoretical piece for the present topic: Bonhoeffer, regularly and rightly interpreted as essentially apolitical, especially in his early thought, infused his inaugural dissertation with the vocabulary of Heidegger. His search for authenticity in faith was associated at an early point with the search for authenticity that would later be understood as a fundamentally political search.

Here, then, an essential recurring motif for this study must be introduced: the idea that, in contrast to commonplace understanding, the crisis of modern civilization that was first embodied in Nazi totalitarianism is not a crisis of "authoritarianism" but, rather, a crisis of authority itself. Put simply, the propensity to totalitarian domination is not a propensity to authoritarianism run rampant, but is rather a potentiality created precisely by the waning of political authority and its substitution by a twisted search for authenticity. This motif requires embellishing in the context of Nazism.

It was Nietzsche who first foresaw the crises that would eventuate in German totalitarianism. Before the turn of the century, he wrote of "what is coming, what can no longer come differently: *the advent of nihilism.*" And juxtaposed with this nihilism was to be a "movement that in some future will take the place of this perfect nihilism—but presupposes it, logically and psychologically, and certainly can come only after and out of it": *the will to power.*[19] It was thus Nietzsche's burden to foresee that authority was crumbling on the Continent at the century's turn, and that what was about to replace it was a dialectic of nihilism and power. That is, where encircling rings of legitimacy once buttressed the practice of power with morality and a sense of social justice, there now would be only amorality and nihilism. And, where the holder of power was once endowed (and constrained) by the traditions of authority, in our future that person would be guided by only the quest for power itself—a quest that, precisely because it is severed from a theory of justice that constitutes the ideological basis of authority, can evidence itself only in domination and destruction: for it affirms nothing. Indeed, it was Nietzsche's call for a "superman" that was perhaps Germany's first cry for a politics built solely on an ethic of personal authenticity.

In German totalitarianism, to which a vulgarized Nietzsche was attached for intellectual legitimacy, we witness the fulfillment of this Nietzschean diagnosis of the modern eclipse of authority. On one hand, there is Hitler and the Nazi party itself. Hitler, who came from outside the authoritarian tradition in German politics, usurped power through violence, appealed to personal authenticity (the "leadership principle"), and wielded power through purges and the fear of purges. The conservatives were not allied with the Nazis. Rather, they backed Hitler only reluctantly, on the assumption that he could be contained by them if he was allowed to hold the reins of power; when such containment proved no longer possible it was the traditional conservatives who spearheaded the political resistance against him.[20] Indeed, the very name of the Nazi party—the National Socialist German Workers Party—represented an attempt to destroy traditional political sensibilities by combining terms of the political Left (socialist, workers) with those of the Right (national, German [having racist overtones during the period]). Hitler, a former itinerant poster-painter whose greatest humiliation had been denial of university admission for the study of art, was in no way an authoritarian leader; he was a uniquely modern breed of tyrant, whose antiauthoritarian quest for personal authenticity resulted in a frustrated creativity manifested in destruction of others and eventually—though the evidence really has been there from the start—the self. On the other hand, the tyranny of a Hitler can develop into modern totalitarianism only when it commands an infrastructure of historically unprecedented technical capabilities and equally unparalleled moral nihilism. Thus, behind Hitler were the "legitimate" businesses who submitted bids for the construction of the gas chambers and the countless technocrats like Adolf Eichmann who, although they never personally killed a Jew, administered the massacre of millions. Such a job is not performed by an authoritarian, but by a nihilist. This historical situation foretold by Nietzche, then, is the context in which Bonhoeffer found himself: the eclipse of authority and its bifurcation into power and nihilism, exacerbated in its destructive potentials by commanding an arsenal of technical capabilities unparalleled in the history of the world.

It is no accident therefore that the legacy of Bonhoeffer embraces the paradox of a man absorbed by a personal religious quest for authenticity who nevertheless finds a way to lodge this search in the political community where authority once stood. For the last hope of the age rested in the interior life where a certain authenticity might be found, and yet the challenge was to prevent the search from degenerating into meaningless self-absorption. As Bonhoeffer put it toward the end of his search, "the most important question . . . is how we can find a basis for human life together, what spiritual realities and laws we accept as the foundation of a meaningful human life," for never before in history have there been people with "so little ground under their feet."[21] This is not the question of an authoritarian or antiauthoritarian; it is the question of a man who acknowledges the collapse of authority and its substitution by an inward spiritual search, but who also realizes that the results of that search must be writ large in order to establish a foundation for social life where none exists. It is this understanding of Bonhoeffer's search that explains why his legacy is so often linked with that of Simone Weil, despite vast differences in the substance of their respective thought. For the paradox of Weil is theoretically identical to Bonhoeffer's: as one of the century's greatest mystics she also was one of the century's most insightful political philosophers. The apparent tension between the two vocations is relaxed when the search for religious authenticity is seen as a response to the collapse of political authority and, perhaps also, as a basis for the new kind of political authority which has yet to emerge. It is the ability of these exemplars to make the search for authenticity political that satisfies our modern thirst for both individuality and community, authenticity and authority.

It follows that one task of Bonhoeffer scholarship is to chronicle his personal religious pilgrimage in an endeavor to make clear the geography of the road he was on and, hence, the plateau he might have reached had he lived to write the treatise on "religionless Christianity." This chronicle, by definition insofar as it is the record of an inward journey, must be psychological.

The Challenge of a Psychological Interpretation

"Nowhere does there exist," concluded Troeltsch in his classic one-thousand-page inquiry into Christian social teachings, "an absolute Christian ethic, which only awaits discovery; all we can do is learn to control the world-situation in its successive phases just as the earlier Christian ethic did in its own way."[22] With these words Troeltsch introduced an idea that religious scholars have almost uniformly accepted as axiomatic ever since: that religious faith must be understood in its social, psychological, and historical context. This is not to say that religious faith may be reduced to its empirical context—that is another argument altogether. But it is to say that the particular form that religious faith takes is subject to interpretation not only in terms of religious content alone but also in terms of the context in which it is embedded and to which it responds.

In supposing that Bonhoeffer's ethic of discipleship may be interpreted biographically—that is, sociopsychologically—I am supposing two things. First, I am positing that discipleship constitutes a religious and normative gestalt of the sort that may rightly be termed an *ethic*. Second, I am positing that the context in which this ethic can be best interpreted is the psychological one of the author's life. Both of these suppositions need to be defended, for it could be argued, on one hand, that *The Cost of Discipleship* does not constitute a coherent Christian ethic but is instead an essentially irrelevant piece of inspirational literature; or, on the other, that even if discipleship can rightly be called an ethic, it does not necessarily follow that it is best interpreted in a psychological context. In the foregoing pages I have suggested the general ways in which discipleship resonates as an ethical gestalt in the context of the challenges of Bonhoeffer's times; what now must be done is to flesh out this meaning of the term *ethic* as well as to give reasons for my placing it in a psychological context.

Twice before in the sociological literature an ethic has been the subject of inquiry, though in one case it was called a "world vision" rather than an ethic. One is Max Weber's study of the Protestant ethic, and the other is Lucien Goldmann's study of the "tragic vision" of Pascal.[23] Now, despite the dissimilarities in approach between the two studies, what is interesting for present purposes is the similarities between the two authors on their understanding of the idea of an ethic. Both consider it, first, to represent a gestalt of material and ideal factors. As Goldmann puts it, "a 'world vision' is the psychic expression of the relationship between certain human groups and their social or physical environment."[24] Such a definition Weber would likely have agreed with, even if Goldmann tends to stress the social determinants of the world vision while Weber tends to stress the ethical determinants of the social situation. Both the agreement and disagreement of the authors is instructive, the result being that we come to understand an ethic as an ideal-material gestalt that is interpretable on either dimension. And thus we begin to see how discipleship may be considered an ethic insofar as it attempts to provide a link between the ideal and the material—that is, between religious faith and the practical implementation of that faith in the praxis of the Christian life. We also see that an interpretation of discipleship may begin on either dimension, depending, as Weber especially stressed, on the questions we set out to address.

But beyond identifying a gestalt of material and ideal factors, both Weber and Goldmann implicitly highlight another crucial aspect of the idea of an ethic. This is that at the core of an ethic lurks a moral paradox of ultimate proportions. To Goldmann, the core of Pascal's tragic vision was nothing less than the paradox of belief in the existence of God, which he could resolve only by the notion of the wager. Of course, the wager does not really resolve the paradox—it is at best a reasonable guess. Thus, the power of the tragic vision resides precisely in the moral paradox it enshrines. Were the paradox to be truly resolved, the moral tension of the vision would dissipate. It is because the tension remains that the vision remains alive and capable of motivating action. A similar paradox underlies Weber's understanding of the Protestant ethic as epitomized by Calvinism. There it was the irresolvable paradox of predestination that constituted the stuff out of which the Protestant ethic drew its capacity to motivate. Ultimately the believer could not know whether he or she was damned or saved, and it was in wrestling with this moral paradox that the Protestant ethic emerged.

In short, an ethic enshrines a moral paradox that it cannot resolve in its own terms, and it is precisely this inability to resolve the paradox that enables the ethic to live as a moral gestalt capable of inspiring action. Discipleship is a preeminent example of an ethic in this sense. Its tension springs from the paradox of obedience to an otherworldly Christ in this world, and it is to wrestle with this paradox that Bonhoeffer bases his *Cost of Discipleship* on a "worldly" interpretation of that most "otherworldly" of all gospel passages, the Sermon on the Mount.

That discipleship is subject to contextual interpretation therefore follows if it is accepted within the definition of an ethic. To the extent that discipleship is regarded as an ethic, it is subject to interpretation in a sociological, psychological, and historical context. An ethic is devised to speak to multiple contexts; its power derives from its redundancy; and it may therefore be fruitfully interpreted from the vantage point of various contexts. Often, moreover, the context which reveals the most about an ethic is not the one to which it speaks overtly. Such is the case with the ethic of discipleship.

It was the political impetus of the ethic of discipleship that initially led scholars down the wrong interpretive path. Specifically, many interpreters have sought to explicate the ethic of discipleship by understanding it as a response to the political context of National Socialism.[25] Yet, increasingly, Bonhoeffer scholars have found this not to have been the biographical case. Instead, they have come to conclude that Bonhoeffer's thought was highly autobiographical, even idiosyncratic, and amazingly apolitical. As a result of this conclusion, most scholars have insisted on the necessity of interpreting Bonhoeffer's thought in a nonpolitical context. Moreover, it has been demonstrated that not even an ecclesiastical context sheds much light on Bonhoeffer's thought, particularly his early thought, because the facts show that prior to 1932 or so Bonhoeffer rarely attended church. Finally, even an intellectual context reveals little about Bonhoeffer, for although he studied with some of the best theological minds of his time, he had an almost uncanny propensity to avoid apprenticeship to strong personalities who might have dominated his intellectual development. To be sure, all of these assertions require qualification— Bonhoeffer did not go completely uninfluenced by the politics of his day, his church, or his teachers—but in terms of substantial influence it is difficult to find primacy in any of these loci. All this is shown clearly in the masterful biography by his student and friend, Eberhard Bethge.[26]

It was in a review of the English edition of that biography that another Bonhoeffer interpreter, John Godsey, raised the question of another context, a sociopsychological one, most forcefully. He queried: "My real question is this, did he do what he did because of his Christian convictions or because of the inbred and inculcated qualities derived from his unusual family?"[27] The question pertains primarily to Bonhoeffer's involvement in the political resistance, and is premised on the biographical observations that Bonhoeffer's opposition to National Socialism was a commitment shared by his entire family, that his family actually preceded him in resistance, that his own role in the conspiracy was made possible by an appointment granted by his brother-in-law Hans von Dohnanyi, that the Berlin home of his parents where he had attic quarters was a center for clandestine conspiratorial discussions, and that when he was executed so also were his brother Klaus, two brothers-in-law, and an uncle. In short, the evidence falls firmly on the side of familial influences, and the suggestion of the appropriate avenue for interpreting the context of Bonhoeffer's thought likewise begins to emerge: that the crucial context must be the sociopsychological one of his family.

All of the evidence that the salient context of Bonhoeffer's life and thought was his family will not be reviewed here, and will be discussed in appropriate places throughout my book. But here it is appropriate to state why I consider the context of the ethic of discipleship to be primarily a psychological—that is a familial— one. The reasons are also provided by Bethge, whose lifelong research on Bonhoeffer has convinced him that all of the central features of discipleship were present in Bonhoeffer's thinking in 1932. As seen by Bethge, this background shows conclusively that *The Cost of Discipleship* could not have emerged in response to the crises of 1933.[28] In other words, according to Bethge, those who interpret *The Cost of Discipleship* as a response to the political challenges of National Socialism are simply and unequivocally wrong. If the ethic of discipleship does have political implications (and I argue that it does), these were not born primarily in a political context. Moreover, as we also know, it was only in 1932 that Bonhoeffer began attending church regularly. Consequently, with neither political nor ecclesiastical influences holding sway over him, only the milieu in which he lived could have constituted the context for the ethic of discipleship, and that milieu was his family.

Finally, as a last bit of biographical evidence suggesting the germinal influence of the sociopsychological context, another item presented by Bethge is worth considering. This is a passage from a sermon in which—amazingly—Bonhoeffer anticipates his own death: "We must not be surprised if once again times return for our Church when the blood of martyrs will be required. But even if we have the courage and faith to spill it, this blood will not be as innocent or as clear as that of the first martyrs. Much of our own guilt will lie in our blood."[29] This passage merits quoting not merely as evidence for the premonition of the disciple about his own death but also because of the date it was preached: 19 June 1932. It, like discipleship itself, could not have arisen in response to Nazi domination. Whatever impelled Bonhoeffer to develop discipleship was not of political but of personal origin.

The present study is not the first to attempt a psychological interpretation of Bonhoeffer's life and thought,[30] although it is the first to make the ethic of discipleship its specific interpretive objective. Moreover, what I have in mind is something quite different from the standard fare of psychological interpretation in Bonhoeffer studies or the psychology of religion generally. At issue here is the problem of reductionism. Without taking specific studies to task and with appreciation for the fact that often their authors do not intend reductionistic conclusions, one must recognize that implicit in the psychological approach is a reductionistic tendency. In the present case, my attempt to articulate the linkages between religious faith and political action by means of a psychological explication of the ethic of discipleship might be construed as implying dominance of psychological processes over either religious faith or political commitment. That would be a wrong conclusion. While I contend that psychological influences were *first* in Bonhoeffer's development, I deny that they were *foremost*. The error of psychological reductionism is seen most dramatically in the moral dissatisfaction we inescapably feel upon witnessing the conclusion: the moral problem under investigation has been resolved by the amoral scientific procedures of psychological investigation. But what we too often fail to see is that, in truth, the moral problem has not been resolved; instead it has been subtly translated into the terms of another domain, the psychological, and *that* problem has been solved. Thus we have the feeling of intellectual satisfaction—the problem has been resolved "elegantly"—but moral dissatisfaction, the moral problem, has not really been touched. The error of this procedure is that a moral problem is supposedly resolved by an amoral discipline, when in reality the beginning problem has been reduced to a lesser one and a strategy appropriate to things has been applied to human affairs.

At issue in a typical psychological interpretation, then, is the subtle bad faith of the psychological investigator. The psychologist (or person employing the tools of psychology) fails to admit that insofar as psychology deals with the "innermost" needs, dispositions, desires, fears, or hopes of a person, it is also dealing with what is "ultimate" to a person and therefore is ipso facto engaged in theologizing. Moreover, insofar as psychology proclaims its theories and findings publicly, the psychologist is engaged in political action and psychology becomes part of the political process. Psychology should, therefore, confront its own role as a moral force; namely, its tacit assumption that the religious and the political may be explained psychologically. If psychology does not confront this moral role, it must be understood as purporting a fundamental irreligious and apolitical view of human nature. In actuality, however, psychology has things backwards. The psychological is the common and relatively mundane soil out of which the unique and moral arises, but it is precisely the germination of human uniqueness that intrigues us. In the present case, it is the unique religious and political ethic of discipleship that we wish to grasp. We cannot do so if we tacitly assume from the beginning that its uniqueness may be accounted for in psychological terms alone.

The task of a psychological interpretation of Bonhoeffer, therefore, is to understand psychological interpretation itself as part of the religious quest and political dialogue. That is, psychology must be understood as a partner in the search for genuine religious faith and responsible political action. This point is especially important to bear in mind given the subject under investigation and the challenges and possibilities it poses to our culture. For in asserting that Bonhoeffer's quest was for authenticity of the sort that could lodge itself into the public community with the hope of establishing new forms of authority, I am indirectly raising the question of the role of introspection, of psychology, in the continuance of western civilization. We are accused today of being "narcissistic,"[31] a "psychological society,"[32] so absorbed with a false sense of an inner life that we are oblivious to politics and, as for religion, have erected an altar of self-worship.[33] The challenge is a real one, and the critique pointed. But I do not think that the solution lies in weaning ourselves from introspection and willy nilly mounting the bandwagon of public commitments in terms defined by outmoded authorities—that is the problem. Rather, the solution lies in challenging psychology to deliver what it promises, to quit cowering beneath the rhetoric of a science more appropriate to things than to people and to become a partner in the search for authentic faith and just authority. In this endeavor to revive psychology from its dogmatic slumber, the trail of intro-spection left by the son of a psychiatrist who himself loathed psychology and favored theology may be a helpful guide.

The psychological framework developed herein is thus con-structed in explicit contrast to traditional psychobiographical stud-ies, and with an open view to the specific moral problem the framework is employed to interpret. It differs from the traditional orientation of such studies, first, by attempting to avoid psycho-logical jargon. However helpful to the specialist, such jargon too often creates the illusion that a labeled psychological state is some-how of greater ontological status than that same state considered in religious, political, or everyday terms. Green, for example, has offered a psychological assessment of Bonhoeffer that finds him to possess a "narcissistic ego."[34] Although I agree with Green's diagnosis, I am disinclined to follow him in the clinical termi-nology for the reason just mentioned.

A second departure of my psychological framework from cer-tain prevailing ones is that I am rejecting the standard typologies of "authoritarian families" and "authoritarian personalities" that have peppered sociopsychological literature for some half a cen-tury. From Lewin's classic study of experimentally created school climates through the vast literature generated by Fromm's *Escape from Freedom* and Adorno and colleagues' *The Authoritarian Per-sonality* to such contemporary family typologies as that presented by Kantor and Lehr's *Inside the Family*,[35] countless publications have asserted more or less the same, generally untested thesis: that authoritarian families produce authoritarian personalities, which in turn become the human stuff of authoritarian political regimes. My patience with this literature is thin. Not only has "narcissism" appeared as an opposing interpretation of the same facts—sometimes from the same scholars themselves[36]—but also the most thorough study of the Nazi youth cohort to date demonstrates that its members simply could not have come from so-called authoritarian backgrounds.[37] Worse, as I have shown, the contemporary political problem is not even authoritarianism, a fact making the assumptions of the entire tradition dubious. And finally, except in the rare cases where the subject is deftly handled, the bulk of this literature contributes to the implicit reductionism that was just criticized. Happily, only one psychological study of Bonhoeffer erred dramatically in this direction, and that was substantially revised prior to publication.[38] But several other studies tacitly embrace it, so it is well to distinguish my orientation from them at the outset.

Last and most important, the psychological framework developed herein begins from the premise that, since it is not the life of a man that interests us so much as an ethic developed in the context of that life, the interpretive framework should not be exclusively psychological but, rather, must itself be essentially moral and, if not political, prepolitical. Put another way, this study is not directed predominantly at Bonhoeffer's interior, psychic life, but at the sociopsychological milieu in which he began to fashion his ethical views. Instead of drawing from a school of psychological thought for my theoretical orientation, I am self-consciously drawing from an emerging perspective in intergenerational family therapy.[39] This perspective explicitly acknowledges the prepolitical status of the family and asserts that the quest for justice is intimately bound up with family life. The idea is that justice often begins in an experience of injustice, and thus has a teleological dimension in the quest for the rectification of injustice in an idealized future world where justice shall reign. Now, this teleological aspect of justice dovetails with the human fact of generations, as parents are inclined to look toward their children for the realization of a more just world. A family ethos emerges, crystallized in the structure of familial authority which the theory of justice establishes, in which children are often "asked" to play predefined parts. The chronicle of Bonhoeffer's development of discipleship is the story of his personal working through of his family's sense of justice as it impinged upon him. This, of course, is important to note as the theoretical backdrop of the story that will unfold. But it is also important to observe that this theoretical orientation differs from psychological interpretation per se in that it comprehends the quest for justice as at once a sociopsychological as well as a religious and political challenge. There is no question of reductionism here; the thread of the same search is merely traced from its prepolitical and prereligious beginnings through its development as a religious ethic with political impetus. Finally, it should be noted that the interpretation developed here has been anticipated by a previous, though less fully developed, interpretation along similar lines.[40] The specific features of the ethic of discipleship must now be presented briefly so that readers are oriented to the specific tasks of my interpretation.

Specific Features of Discipleship

The appeal of an ethic to the emotions, its capacity to motivate where rational argument alone falls short, and indeed its praxic nature, as I have said, derives from the fact that at the existential core of an ethic is a paradox of ultimate proportions which reason alone cannot resolve. Hence, an ethic is born which enshrines that paradox in such a way that only thought *and* action—praxic faith if you will—is deemed adequate to wrestling with the ultimate questions that are shrouded in paradox. It follows that an ethic has both a history and a teleology. One can trace the emergence of an ethic by discovering in the life of the ethic's originator or of the people who embrace the ethic those ideas and circumstances that first raised the unresolvable questions that then led to the crafting of the ethic. In addition, one may follow the ethic through its "life" until the point is reached where the paradoxes of the ethic "explode" in action that then demolishes the ethic, perhaps not so much by resolving the paradoxes of the ethic as by robbing them of their existential force through enacting them in history. In this study of discipleship, the bulk of the effort will be directed toward tracing the emergence of the ethic in its originator's life. However, as was mentioned at the outset and as will be considered again in the concluding chapter, some attention is also paid to the resolution of the ethic of discipleship in Bonhoeffer's political resistance to German totalitarianism.

In order to provide my interpretation of the ethic of discipleship, I must from the outset be as clear as possible regarding the specific paradoxical features that constitute discipleship and so make it an ethic. The plural "paradoxes" is used because, although in general discipleship enshrines only the age-old paradox of following an otherworldly Christ in this world, scrutinized more closely, discipleship can be said to contain no less than three different paradoxes, which, taken together, constitute what is unique about Bonhoeffer's ethic of discipleship. Here I want to describe briefly each of these paradoxes. Each one will then be considered more or less independently in the three chapters that follow.

The three paradoxes that constitute the ethic of discipleship concern, for lack of better terms, the sociality of Christ, costly grace, and obedience. By understanding the formation and progression of each of these—from the family context in which they were born to the political context in which they were lodged—we will be in a position to comprehend the search that Bonhoeffer called "discipleship." Now, it must be clear that in characterizing discipleship by means of these three paradoxes, I am carving out an interpretation of a sociological rather than a theological nature. My reading of the theological literature interpreting discipleship suggests to me that my interpretation is not in opposition to this; but it is different. I want to cull from discipleship the sociological features that constitute its ethical nature, and this, of necessity, puts the present exposition on a somewhat different track from what a theological one might take. But, again, I do not think my interpretation opposes a theological one so much as it merely organizes the lines of interpretation differently—along their paradoxical axes.

The Sociality of Christ

Throughout all of Bonhoeffer's thought runs a conception of faith as a fundamentally social enterprise. Because this conception is found as either a proposition or a premise in all his thought, it is the element least unique to discipleship. And because the theological argument for the sociality of faith was rationally articulated as early as 1927 in his dissertation, it is also the least paradoxical intellectually of all the features of discipleship. It does, however, become paradoxical when the problem becomes one of action rather than thought alone, but first let us understand Bonhoeffer's intellectual commitment to sociality.

Bonhoeffer's dissertation, *The Communion of Saints*, which he submitted to the theological faculty of the University of Berlin at the precocious age of twenty-one, presents his understanding of the social dimensions of faith in arguments that, in the main, he never departed from later. Trained in the liberal theological tradition of the Berlin establishment, Bonhoeffer in *The Communion of Saints* takes as his task the reconciling of Barth's notion of the Word of God addressing persons freely from the outside with propositions about humankind's essentially social nature derived from both the liberal school of theology and the emerging social sciences generally. Despite the complexities of an often obscure and always turgid discussion, and despite his dubious handling of the theories of several classical sociological thinkers,[41] the brilliance of the argument resides in his definition of the person in terms that would be acceptable to virtually all social psychologists today, as well as liberal theologians. He views the person as essentially a social entity, suspended in interaction with others and therefore embedded in community. It follows that when the person of God addresses the person of man, he does so corporately or socially. Again, this is so by definition, for the person cannot be understood atomistically but only socially. Ergo, the Word is always addressed to man in community, and faith is fundamentally a social enterprise. Therefore, when Bonhoeffer considers the doctrine of the church, which is his overt theme in *The Communion of Saints*, he concludes that, as the receptacle of the Word on earth, "the church is Christ existing as community." The proposition, often repeated by Bonhoeffer in this and later works, simply signifies that sociality, the essence of personhood, is also the essence of faith. Observe that there is no question of an immanent or transcendental (in the Kantian sense) spirituality welling up from the community itself: the community is always the gracious recipient of a Word that is spoken where it will. But at the same time, the Word is not spoken to atomized, individualistic man, but to a community of persons, a church. Considering this theme, one is not surprised that when Barth finally read it years later, he remarked that *The Communion of Saints* was a "theological miracle."[42] Essentially Barthian, it set as its task the fleshing out of the underemphasized social dimension in neo-orthodoxy, which on the whole it achieved successfully.

It is thus that the Word, spoken and received in community, became the cornerstone of all of Bonhoeffer's later thought. At first, one witnesses this commitment of Bonhoeffer's in the emphasis he places on sermons in his 1928 pastoral apprenticeship in Barcelona. For him, the sermon preached in the church is in fact the Word of God. This is why he memorized his sermons before delivery and why he urged his students to do the same. This is also why he took the pronouncements made in both the German churches and the ecumenical movement with such seriousness (and why he fought the nazification of the churches so ardently): what was pronounced in Christian community was to be taken literally as the revelation of God. But also, one witnesses this commitment of Bonhoeffer's to sociality in the kinds of work he chose to undertake as a student and pastor. During his postdoctoral studies in New York in 1930–31, for example, it was to a black church in Harlem that he chose to commit himself. Perhaps not incidentally, it was there that he acquired a liking for American Negro spirituals and began to develop quite a private record collection comprised of them, even though he loathed the music in mainstream American churches, considering it a detraction. Then, too, we see Bonhoeffer's commitment to the sociality of faith when, upon his return to Germany, he took charge of a rowdy confirmation class in a working-class district of Berlin— and voluntarily moved into the same neighborhood and, via group activities, suggested the commitment to communal living that he later developed. And finally, it is his commitment to the social dimensions of the faith that lurks behind the intellectual's dissatisfaction with university teaching and his desire for practical Christian work which eventually took him to Finkenwalde, which was established for the practical portion of pastoral training, and to the experiments of the disciple with communal living that he would attempt there.

In his thought, too, the commitment to sociality continues. Against the advice of his dissertation director, Reinhold Seeberg, who suggested that church history was a relatively open field for a budding theologian of his talents, Bonhoeffer continued to think sociologically and philosophically in his inaugural dissertation, *Act and Being*, where he reiterated his thesis that "the church is Christ existing as community." Later, in his 1938 *Life Together,* the theological proposition is uttered entirely practically: "God has willed," he writes, "that we should seek and find His living Word in the witness of a brother, in the mouth of man."[43] And between these two is, of course, discipleship. Discipleship is premised on the assumption, rooted in the Sermon on the Mount, that following Christ is identical with serving others in Christian integrity. One does turn the other cheek and walk the extra mile, and that is obedience to Christ. Indeed, the previously quoted passage suggesting that the disciple may be asked to follow Christ out of the monastery and into the world is premised on the assumption that faith is not a private, individualistic entity but a corporate reality. Although the argument in *The Cost of Discipleship* is not developed within its pages, as happens in other of Bonhoeffer's earlier and later writings, it is premised on a notion of the fundamentally social nature of faith and the Christian life.

How then is the notion of the sociality of Christ paradoxical? It is not immediately. Rather, at least initially it is a quite sensible conclusion from reflection upon certain sociopsychological and theological concerns. Moreover, as Bethge and others have commented, Bonhoeffer was reared in an atmosphere that stressed humanistic values and, when he took them over into theology, he was simply expressing a "Christian humanism" for which "solidarity with humanity" was merely a central tenet.[44] This is all true. But the paradox emerges when the commitment to humanity runs counter to other, equally compelling commitments. In Bonhoeffer's case, the paradox arose in the concrete on the matter of "the Jewish Question." Commitment to humanity included Jews, first his friend Franz Hildebrandt, who was barred from his ministry early in the Nazi regime because of his Jewish origins and the Aryan Clauses that prohibited Jews from holding civil office, which included the ministry; later his twin sister, who was married to a Jew and whom Bonhoeffer consequently had to escort to the Swiss border in the thick of night in 1938; and ultimately to Jews in general. For ultimately, as he is said to have put it to his Finkenwalde students, "he who does not cry out for the Jews cannot sing

Gregorian chants!"[45] But in the political circumstances of the time, to hold such a view was also ipso facto to engage in political resistance, and the paradox was that Christian faith was forcing Bonhoeffer into direct confrontation with the state. And indeed, the first clandestine act of political resistance in which Bonhoeffer participated, "Operation 7," was a plot to save seven Jews by arranging their illegal emigration. It was thus at this juncture—when his sense of obligation to obey the state, derived from theological principles, ran counter to his commitment to human-ity, also derived from theological principles—that the sociality of Christ forced Bonhoeffer into a paradox. In truth, the paradox is an imposed one—imposed everywhere that governments violate human rights—rather than one chiseled uniquely into the ethic of discipleship. Interpretive attention must therefore be focused more strongly on the other two paradoxes of discipleship, although the sociality of Christ must always be remembered to be the paradoxical context in which the other two are embedded.

Costly Grace

"Cheap Grace is the deadly enemy of our Church. We are fighting to-day for costly grace."[46] So begins the first chapter of *The Cost of Discipleship*. And in contrast to "cheap grace," "costly grace is the treasure hidden in the field." It is "*costly* because it calls us to follow, and it is *grace* because it calls us to follow *Jesus Christ*."[47] In this metaphorical opposition between cheap and costly grace, Bonhoeffer self-consciously erects the paradox with which he wishes to introduce discipleship. To be sure, it was only toward the end of his teaching and reflection upon discipleship that he developed this metaphor and the paradox with which to inau-gurate it—as if he had finally found the paradoxical core of the ethic and so was free to unleash it—although it is central to the ethic of discipleship psychologically and politically.[48]

Actually, the metaphor of costly grace encapsulates two paradoxes, both of which I will consider under the heading of costly grace. The first is the most obvious. It is that, most profoundly, the "cost" of grace is the absolute one: death. Throughout *The Cost of Discipleship* Bonhoeffer returns to the theme of death— we have already seen the most-quoted instance, where he writes that "when Christ calls a man he bids him to come and die." Of course, by this Bonhoeffer is recalling via allusion the biblical passage in which Jesus, too, and later Paul, asserts that for a person to be "alive" in Christ he must be "dead" to sin. By choosing the theme of death to suggest the ultimate "price" of grace, he is therefore on solid biblical grounds. But he is also on solid biographical grounds. As shall be shown in Chapter III, not only was literal death an impetus for Bonhoeffer's theological and ethical career, but also it is the theme of death to which he returns again and again (often enough for one interpreter to accuse him of having a "death wish"[49]). Indeed, there will be various opportunities to use Bonhoeffer's meditations on death as occasions for deeper understanding of the ethic of discipleship, but for now we should simply understand the paradox of costly grace to be that historic Christian paradox of "life" being granted only through "death." It is a paradox to assert, as does Bonhoeffer, that grace is "costly because it costs a man his life, and it is grace because it gives a man the only true life."[50] And it is this paradox that stands on the opening page of *The Cost of Discipleship*.

More subtle but equally profound is the rational paradox suggested by the metaphor of cheap and costly grace. This paradox is that the metaphor is established only to be shattered. Bonhoeffer does not mean by costly grace that grace is merely very expensive; he means that it is of infinite value. By employing metaphors from the marketplace, where, as Marx observed, "use value" becomes transformed through the quantitative manipulations of the price system into "exchange value," Bonhoeffer is most fundamentally suggesting the inapplicability of a quantitative rationality applied to grace. Grace has only use value; to think of it as having exchange value, as a spiritual technique, is to miss its point. True grace meets man only at the end of his reasoning powers, where quantitative, technical, calculative rationality passes its limit. Indeed, it is just this kind of limited reasoning, when applied to grace, that Bonhoeffer calls "cheap grace"—"grace sold on the market like cheapjacks' wares," which

> means grace as a doctrine, a principle, a system. It means forgiveness of sins proclaimed as a general truth, the love of God taught as the Christian "conception" of God. An intellectual assent to that idea is held to be of itself sufficient to secure remission of sins. . . . In such a Church the world finds a cheap covering for its sins; no contrition is required, still less any real desire to be delivered from sin. Cheap grace therefore amounts to a denial of the living Word of God, in fact, a denial of the Incarnation of the Word of God.[51]

Therefore, it is the very metaphor of cheap and costly grace that Bonhoeffer explicates by stretching it to its breaking point. Cheap grace is the grace calculated by human reason, and so an impostor. Costly grace, true grace, is the gratuitous gift of God that finds man only where man cannot find himself. And this is the paradox of costly grace: that only when our efforts have failed at achieving grace through our own reason do we meet grace at a place beyond our cognitive faculties. Finally, it is only to cheap grace that "an intellectual assent" can be appropriately made; as for costly grace, the stuff of the ethic of discipleship, it is a paradox which a person cannot fathom but only appreciate and obey.

Paradox of Obedience

Discipleship, of course, literally means obedience, and the German title of *The Cost of Discipleship*, *Nachfolge*, suggests just this: "following after" might be a literal translation. But obedience, whether religious or other, is a problem-ridden construct.

One may obey an external authority—and become subject to the charge of authoritarianism by those who do not accept that authority. Or one may choose to obey some inner standard—but this approach leaves one wide open to the accusation of solipsism or, worse, insanity. The challenge of obedience, then, especially in modern times that have witnessed the collapse of authority and the quest for authenticity, is to be obedient to an inner sense which nevertheless can be shown (or argued) to have ontological status outside oneself. And when the construct at issue is—as it is here—authentic religious faith, the problem of obedience necessarily raises the question of the existence of God. For—outside of the authority of established religious traditions unquestionably accepted—how do we know that God exists? The problem of religious obedience has had this question as its focal point ever since the slow process of secularization set in centuries ago. And it of course was the central paradox of Pascal's "tragic vision." The question arises, therefore, of how an ethic of radical Christian obedience in the modern world—discipleship—resolves this problem of the existence of God. In this question is what is here termed the "paradox of obedience."

Bonhoeffer's confrontation with this obstacle is a bold one: he ignores it! He writes, simply but surely, "*only he who believes is obedient, and only he who is obedient believes.*"[52] In other words, he refuses to deal with the problem of disbelief, but construes it as a problem of obedience. Belief, he asserts, will follow from obedience, as obedience then follows from belief; the two are inseparable. Echoing the juxtaposition of faith and works in James, he leaves little doubt that this paradox of obedience and belief is a part of his metaphor of costly grace: presumably, belief and obedience can be distinguished only when one fails to appreciate the ultimate dimensions of the problem and subsumes them under human rationality. Nevertheless, in any ordinary scheme of things (and we must assume that Bonhoeffer, too, was an ordinary human being), this assertion is paradoxical. Moreover, in addition to the fact of the paradox, its nature betrays the ethical dimensions of discipleship, for the paradox of obedience is nothing less than a call to commitment and action. Not content with the more resigned wager, Bonhoeffer takes the problem of belief to be an occasion for ethical risk.

This paradox of obedience will be discussed more fully in Chapter IV, but there is one thing that can be anticipated from it now. From the paradox of obedience Bonhoeffer evidently saw an ordering to events: that *if* one obeys, *then* one will believe. My inference is that discipleship revealed some struggle that Bonhoeffer was straining to conquer by means of a single-minded obedience, that he was refusing to question his obedience until he had resolved the struggle. And indeed there was a struggle, a family struggle, and only when Bonhoeffer joined his family in the resistance—only when he followed obedience into death— was he freed from that struggle and from the burden of discipleship. Only then was he freed for a new kind of faith, a "religionless" faith in a "world come of age." Indeed, in the 1944 letter in which he first mentions his reservations about *The Cost of Discipleship*, he provides a synopsis of his error as being that he thought he could acquire faith "by living a holy life, or something like it."[53] Here Bonhoeffer lends support to my hypothesis of the twofold significance of the paradox of obedience. On one hand, it was a genuine paradox energizing an ethic. But on the other hand, there was a chronology to it. Through obedience he thought he could acquire faith. It is the task of the rest of this study to chronicle his quest in the context of the arena in which the injunction to obey was first heard: the prepolitical, prereligious arena of the family.

II

Sociality and Family

"The only sociological category that could possibly be compared to the church," Bonhoeffer wrote in his doctoral dissertation is "the original patriarchal structure of the family. The father's will is that his children and servants live in community, and obedience to the father consists in preserving this community. That is why the image of the family occurs so frequently in the Christian vocabulary, and has given us the most usual New Testament name which Christians call each other, namely 'brother.' "[1] A wealth of insight about both the social context of Bonhoeffer's thought and its character is revealed in this comparison drawn by the twenty-one-year-old theology student. To be sure, the comparison that Bonhoeffer himself called "approximate" should not be pressed by later interpreters into a proposition so bold as Day's contention that Bonhoeffer's description of the church is nothing but a description of his own family.[2] Yet the comparison is drawn by Bonhoeffer, and it is a fact that during the twenty-odd years that preceded its writing he only infrequently attended the actual church about which he ostensibly wrote. Thus, the comparison is suggestive, if not conclusive, about the social context of Bonhoeffer's thought and the roots of his commitment to sociality.

The task of this chapter is to flesh out this comparison between family and ecclesiology in Bonhoeffer's own life and thought. Specifically, I wish to introduce the Bonhoeffer family descriptively so that readers can become acquainted with its members and atmosphere. Next, I want to present the essential evidence for considering the family to be the primary social context out of which Bonhoeffer's thought arose. This presentation will involve briefly sketching the coordinates of Bonhoeffer's biography with an eye to the people and contexts which likely held sway over him. Lastly, I want to begin the interpretive work by wrestling with the problem of the relationship between the structure of the Bonhoeffer family and the character of Dietrich Bonhoeffer's commitment to sociality in his thought. In short, I want to begin the search for isomorphisms between social practice and social thought. Later chapters dealing with more discrete features of discipleship will be more specific in tracing the chronological emergence of the ethic of discipleship.

To prevent misunderstanding, though, and also to anticipate my argument, one feature of the above-quoted comparison between family and church should be noted straightaway. This is that Bonhoeffer draws his comparison not between the church and any family, but between the church and a specific type of family: "the original patriarchal structure of the family," as he puts it. This is interesting both for what it says and what it fails to say. It says that the family structure Bonhoeffer has in mind is one that, as shall be shown, was very much like his own, but also one that has all but vanished from the west today, and not without applause from some quarters. From this comparison, superficially considered, we might unwittingly prepare ourselves for interpretations and arguments along the standard patriarchal-authoritarian axis. But there is a second aspect of this comparison drawn by Bonhoeffer, conspicuous in its absence, that should prepare us for a wholly different line of interpretation. This is that, in his brief description of the patriarchal family, Bonhoeffer mentions the father, children, and even servants—but not the mother. Her absence is glaring, especially since one would think that, in Bonhoeffer's understanding of the family, she would be the person who would contribute most to the preservation of the community in obedience to the father. Her omission suggests that it is the author himself who has taken on her role and so feels no need to mention her in the text. Indeed, the role Bonhoeffer takes for himself as sociologist of the church is pre-eminently that of obeying the father by seeking to preserve the community. In familial terms, it is the role of the children, the servants, and—mostly—the mother. Ergo, the mother is not actually absent from the quotation but is there implicitly in the role of the author. Armed with the suspicion that Bonhoeffer's commitment to sociality is anchored in an alliance between himself and his mother, we are in a position to avoid certain interpretive pitfalls and to anticipate the unfolding of Bonhoeffer's story.

The Bonhoeffer Family

Dietrich Bonhoeffer was born on 4 February 1906, in Breslau. He was forced to share the limelight of infancy with a twin sister, Sabine, and had been preceded by three brothers and two sisters. A healthy baby, Dietrich would grow up in "a family that derived its real education, not from school, but from a deeply-rooted sense of being guardians to a great historical heritage and intellectual tradition."[3] That he could complete his doctorate at age twenty-one was only partly because of his own exceptional ability, for he also had every advantage that rearing, heritage, and wealth could provide.

In this sketch of the Bonhoeffers, I begin with the family heritage.

The Heritage

The Bonhoeffers were a family of goldsmiths and theologians and, later, of lawyers and doctors, whose roots since 1513 had been in Schwäbisch-Hall and prior to that in Holland. Friedrich E. P. T. Bonhoeffer (1828–1907), Dietrich's grandfather, had been president of the High Court at Tübingen when he died. His conservatism, however, was partially diluted by his wife, Julie Bonhoeffer, née Tafel (1842–1936), who had come from somewhat more liberal circles. It was this grandmother with whom Dietrich stayed in Tübingen during his first year of university studies, and it was she who implanted in him the urge to visit Gandhi, as she felt that Dietrich should take every opportunity available to temper his western religiosity with the great traditions of the east. More generally, the two had a warm relationship throughout her life. It was this grandmother who, at age ninety-one, barged through the Nazi blockade of Jewish shops in order to make a purchase and a point.

On Dietrich's mother's side of the family, there were two distinct heritages. The first of these were the von Hases. Dietrich's maternal grandfather was Karl Alfred von Hase (1842–1914), professor of practical theology at Breslau and member of the Supreme Church Council. Since Professor von Hase died in the year that Dietrich turned eight, it is doubtful that there was much direct influence between grandfather and grandson. Still, it was in the von Hases that the study of theology and service in the church touched most directly upon the Bonhoeffer family of Dietrich's generation. Typically, when the Bonhoeffers engaged the services of a clergyman for an obligatory religious ceremony, it was a member of the von Hase family who so served. And, it was well remembered by the Bonhoeffers that Karl August von Hase (1800–1890), Dietrich's great-grandfather, had been more than an outstanding church historian. He had also been something of a political rabble-rouser who had found himself imprisoned for a time by the king of Württemberg—a fate, as chance would have it, that he had shared with a member of the Tafel family. This dovetailing of genealogies undoubtedly tickled the Bonhoeffers, who, though not people to flaunt their aristocratic heritage, were a family who enjoyed a hint of folly encroaching upon an otherwise sedate lineage. Indeed, they appeared more prone to appreciate a good joke than to celebrate the memory of a bygone relative. All the same, the heritage was there.

The third relatively independent strand of heritage for the Bonhoeffer family was that traceable to Dietrich's maternal grandmother, Clara von Hase, née Countess Kalckreuth (1851–1903). She had herself been a gifted musician, and Bethge reports that her father and brother were among the greatest German painters of the nineteenth century. It was to this influence that the Bonhoeffer's traced son Dietrich's budding gift for music, which he evidenced at an early age by becoming an accomplished pianist. Because of chronology, there was no direct influence between this grandmother and Dietrich, but there is little question that he, along with his parents and siblings, perceived himself to have an eye and ear for the arts. Indeed, evenings in the Bonhoeffer home were often enlivened by music-making, and the corridors of their residence were punctuated by not a few notable works of art. To oversimplify: whereas the Bonhoeffers contributed scholarship and professionalism to the family, and the von Hases contributed an ethical and religious sensitivity, Clara von Hase contributed the aesthetic sense that wove it all together in a polyphonic unity.

But what heritage had bestowed, money and training nurtured. In 1912 Karl Bonhoeffer, Dietrich's father, was appointed professor of psychiatry and neurology at the University of Berlin—the most esteemed position of its kind in Germany. For the Bonhoeffer children, and Dietrich, who was ten at the time, this elevation meant that they would grow up in the Grünewald district of Berlin, something of a professors' quarter. There, until 1935, the family came to be on friendly terms with some of Germany's most distinguished scholars, such as Max Planck, Adolf von Harnack, and Ernst Troeltsch. Years later the family would remember with fondness the Wednesday-evening discussions at the home of the historian Delbrück, where Theodore Heuss, the future president of the Federal Republic, put in an occasional appearance. For their part, the Bonhoeffers also did their share of entertaining, and, especially during Dietrich's student years at the University of Berlin, their Grünewald home was the not infrequent scene of parties hosted by the seven Bonhoeffer children and their spouses or spouses-to-be. But, as we have seen, guests were not a requirement for an evening of merriment at the Bonhoeffer home, since all of the children had mastered either a musical instrument or the art of singing, and many an evening passed with the traditional German enthusiasm for music-making. Dietrich was the family pianist, and he is remembered especially for his tireless and skillful accompaniment even when it encroached upon his own practice time.

It is difficult to appreciate by today's standards the grandeur of the Grünewald home—or the one before it in Breslau—or the fact that it was not ostentatious by the standards of the surrounding community. It had room enough for parents, eight children, and five servants, for Dr. Bonhoeffer's study—and at Breslau for a schoolroom as well as separate boys' and girls' play rooms—and still room to spare for visiting relatives, including, in one case, an entire family. Photographs of particular rooms reveal a lavish expansiveness which finds, as one commentator puts it, a grand piano as but an "agreeable incident."[4] Then, too, there was a country home at Friedrichsbrunn, purposely never wired for electricity, where the children could cultivate the German love of nature and romp in woods and water.

Obviously, the Bonhoeffers did not want for money or material goods. In his adult years, Dietrich would even worry that perhaps he had been too fortunate as a child, and that this privilege prevented him from truly understanding the plight of the masses. Indeed, even when the inflation reached its peak in 1923 and 1924 and everyone felt its impact, the Bonhoeffers were spared the worst because Karl Bonhoeffer had a sufficient number of foreign patients who paid him in a more stable foreign currency. Moreover, it is almost commonplace to note the humility of the Bonhoeffer parents, who never discussed financial matters with their children and refused to allow them to flaunt their wealth.

The Bonhoeffers did make a sincere effort to temper their own financial security with humanitarian ideals. The children were required to treat others with the same courtesy that they felt entitled to and never to use wealth as a measure of character. The Bonhoeffers' doors were always open to needy friends and relatives. Sabine reports an incident during which a prowler was caught in their home and, rather than running him off, their mother offered him a meal. In like manner, Dietrich is said to have been quite generous with his money, offering it freely to friends in need.

The Parents

Against this impressive backdrop towered the authoritarian but gentle patriarch, Karl Bonhoeffer (1868–1948). A man of profound learning and professional repute, he is nevertheless remembered as having been kind and sincere. It is difficult to capture an honest picture of this man. On one hand there are judgments like those of Day, who provides a scathing indictment of the authoritarianism of this patriarch.[5] To be sure, there is some substance to Day's assessment. Karl Bonhoeffer's word, admittedly infrequent, was never questioned in the home—or probably outside of it as well. Whereas Paula Bonhoeffer, the children's mother, enjoyed considerable freedom and independence—as did the children—there is no question that Dr. Bonhoeffer's word was the last one, should he choose to speak it. As for the children, they were not allowed to speak at mealtimes unless spoken to, and spoken to they often were: their father would put to them a question, and their task was to respond in crisp, clear German without the usage of any "hollow phrases" which their father so detested. There is a report, for example, of Dietrich, barely twelve and immersed in the classics, mispronouncing a word, only to be greeted with hearty and embarrassing laughter. The standards that Dr. Bonhoeffer held for his children were incredibly high, and he was not lax in enforcing them. And, to complete the picture of authoritarianism, it appears that the father, immersed in his work, had very little time for his children except to set—and enforce—the standards by which they would be reared.

Despite the truth in this picture of Dr. Bonhoeffer's authoritarianism, however, it is most likely a one-sided one. Probably more realistic is Bethge's view that "from a modern standpoint their upbringing was probably 'authoritarian,' since the parents' word was never questioned, but by the standard of the time it was fairly liberal."[6] That is, Karl Bonhoeffer may have been "remote and reserved," as Sabine puts it, "yet when he looked at anyone his eyes were full of intense understanding. If he wanted to emphasize some point he did so by intonation and never by raising his voice."[7] His authoritarianism was, to say the least, tempered with compassion. The extent of the punishment he leveled on his children was that of a lowered eyebrow. Never striking or shouting at his children, he commanded from them sufficient respect to be able to make his point with a slight facial expression or a brief phrase. Moreover, although each child was compelled to excel, each was also left entirely free to choose the area in which he or she would work. And, as for scorn toward the "hollow phrase," it was more than a pedagogic technique; it was also reflective of the ethical ideals with which the children were faced: just as language should be clear and to the point, so also trivial matters about another's person, such as appearance or wealth, had no place in human discourse. The closest a Bonhoeffer child was allowed to come to commenting on another's attractiveness, for example, was to say that so-and-so has a "nice expression." To say more about such trivial matters would be to employ a "hollow phrase." Thus, we see that underlying Karl Bonhoeffer's so-called authoritarianism was, in fact, a bedrock of humanitarian ideals. If he was the kind who, as Scheller says, "utterly disliked all that is immoderate, exaggerated or undisciplined, [and] so too, in his own person everything was completely controlled,"[8] this austerity was always put in the service of human dignity. The Bonhoeffer children, granted the right to their own opinions, were nevertheless reared by their father to respect the right of others to hold theirs. This, of course, was all taught in an authoritarian context, but the essence of that context worked against its becoming rank tyranny and endowed it with legitimacy. It was this endowment that distinguished Karl Bonhoeffer's character from the kind of authoritarianism that Day attributes to him. Put another way, if the father's word was the *cantus firmus* of the Bonhoeffer household, it allowed for many a counterpointed melody.

One of these counterpointed melodies was the personality of Paula Bonhoeffer (1876–1951). Although Thielicke's phrase "blue-aproned categorical imperative" was not applied to her, it is commonly brought up when discussing her. Bethge remarks that there were some who suspected that she "wore the trousers" in the family. Most clearly supportive of this opinion are facts such as Paula Bonhoeffer's fight to be the first woman to gain the right of establishing her own school, a fight in which she was successful. Then, too, there is the simple fact that running the Bonhoeffer household was itself no small chore, since it included command-ing five servants, eight children and later their spouses, and often relatives and friends. Franz Hildebrandt, Dietrich's friend, for example, writes of the Bonhoeffer household as his second home "by grace and adoption."[9] Surely many others felt this way as well. Finally, there is the sense one gleans from the biographies that Karl Bonhoeffer was often a shadowy figure in the household, tucked away in his study for long hours immersed in work. This paternal habit left Paula Bonhoeffer with the sole task of admin-istering the large and diverse household, and it was around her that it appears to have revolved.

There is little doubt that the children's world was centered on their mother. Again, the Bonhoeffer home was a self-contained social unit, leaving little cause for especially a young child to venture out. And the children appeared to have little desire to do so either. All reports suggest that Paula Bonhoeffer filled the home with such comfortable warmth that, if learning was all that was allowed to go on within the schoolroom, there were plenty of less confining activities going on outside the schoolroom. For example, the children would often write, direct, and perform plays within the home—with their mother as a delighted participant. As the children matured, both play and plays gave way to the aforementioned student parties and evenings of musical enter-tainment, and Paula Bonhoeffer appears again to have played a central role. A pious woman (and a von Hase), she saw no need to send her children out for religious instruction but undertook the task herself—with methods that son Dietrich would later copy when put in charge of religious instruction. A compassionate

woman, she is said to have wept when her children wept and to
have borne the burdens of their friends willingly. Gifted in song,
she instilled in her children an appreciation of those things which
were not quite understandable to her scientifically trained and
empirically inclined husband. An independent woman, she helped
her children believe in themselves enough to make difficult decisions that went against prevailing cultural currents. Nowhere is
there a disparaging word to be found about her, and none seems
deserved.

What then, do we make of the authority structure of the Bonhoeffer family? With each parent strong in respective spheres, it
is difficult to place them in one or another simplistic mold. Instead,
it appears that Sabine's description of Christmas Eve in the Bonhoeffer family—a description that more will be made of later—
best captures the dual structure of authority in this family.[10] Sabine's
recollection is this: on Christmas Eve the children would gather
around their mother, who would read to them the Christmas story
from the Bible. But as she would read, she would be overcome
by the impact of the story and would begin to cry. Listening
attentively, the children would begin to feel uneasy at the sight
of their mother in tears. Then, unnoticed—and it is interesting
that he could manage to go so unnoticed—the children's father
would have slipped out and lit the Christmas candles. The uneasiness would then give way to hymns, led by their mother, and
this would be followed by the joyful opening of presents. In this
way, the authority of mother and father would gently complement
one another. From their mother the children learned the traditional nineteenth-century feminine virtues of faith, morality, community, and song; from their father they learned the nineteenth-
century masculine role at its best: strong yet caring, authoritarian
yet gentle and humane. And all reports indicate that mother and
father loved each other deeply and so provided the children with
a secure home that neither parent alone could have provided.

The Children

According to their seventh child, the eight Bonhoeffer children were perceived to be divided into three groups.[11] The first group was the "three big boys": Karl-Friedrich (1899–1957), Walter (1899–1918), and Klaus (1901–1945). Karl-Friedrich was the firstborn, who, true to speculation about such matters, became the most like his father in disposition. An internationally acclaimed physicist, he was paid this tribute by his colleagues, in words that might have applied as well to his father: "in the most difficult times he remained completely objective and upheld truth throughout."[12] The First World War, in which he served and was wounded, led him to become something of a socialist, but it was probably only in this respect that he rebelled from his father's tutelage. In other respects he remained committed to empiricism, agnosticism, and humanism. At thirty he married Grete von Dohnanyi, with whom he fathered four children. Little is recorded about Karl-Friedrich's role in the resistance, and it is likely that it was minimal.

Walter was the second of the three older boys. Born prematurely at seven months, he is said to have been slighter in build than Karl-Friedrich and to have resembled his mother. A sensitive child whose love of nature was unflagging and led him to dabble in zoology along with his sister Christine, he was especially close to his mother. It was a crushing blow to both mother and father when, in April 1918, Walter died of wounds received in the war.

Klaus, the third of the three older boys, eventually became a respected lawyer despite his distaste for school. He is remembered by Sabine to have had a keen sense of fairness matched by a hot temper. It was probably this temper, combined with Klaus's premonitions of death, which caused Hans von Dohnanyi to prefer Dietrich to Klaus as a confidant in conspiratorial discussions, though it was undoubtedly Klaus's commitment to justice that allowed him to withstand torture at the hands of the Gestapo and the temptation to take his own life. At twenty-nine he married Emmi Delbrück and they had three children. In 1945 his life was cut short when he was executed by the Nazis.

These, then, were the "three big boys." According to Sabine, it was they "who in many respects provided our standards and set the tone for us."[13] On the one hand, they espoused the values of their parents' world: discipline, objectivity, skepticism, humanism. Yet, having experienced the horrors of the world's first total war firsthand, they were in some respects more cynically wise than were their parents. To be sure, Dietrich's relationship with these brothers must have been what he had in mind in his 1933 talk on the leadership principle, for he went to considerable lengths to distinguish not only the older from the younger generation but also those in the younger generation who had experienced the war and those who had not.[14] Moreover, because none of these elder Bonhoeffer children espoused any religious interest, many commentators believe that Dietrich's lifelong dialogue with the world was, in large part, a continuation of his childhood debates with these brothers.

Following the three older boys came the "two girls," Ursula (b. 1902) and Christine (1903–1965). Their story, to be frank, is a story of how they married: the task of a Bonhoeffer daughter was to marry, and marry well. This they both did, Ursula to Rüdiger Schleicher (sacrificing her own studies in social work) and Christine to Hans von Dohnanyi (sacrificing her studies in zoology). These brothers-in-law were welcomed into the circle of Bonhoeffer children and, as will be seen, each was killed by the Nazis in 1945.

The final group of Bonhoeffer children consisted of "the twins," Dietrich and Sabine (b. 1906), together with a baby sister, Susanne (b. 1909). Sabine married Gerhard Leibholz, a lawyer whose Jewish ancestry forced the couple and their children to move in 1938 to London, where they stayed in exile for nearly a decade. About

Susanne little is reported except for her marriage to Walter Dress, a pastor and friend of Dietrich's from his student days, and the fact of her and her husband's successful efforts at assisting Jews in hiding during the Third Reich. Dietrich was the elder of the twins by ten minutes, a fact which Sabine remembers him reminding her of a bit too often. Even so, Sabine remembers him—with a ring of authenticity—as having been a sensitive and even chivalrous boy who went out of his way to see that his sister had just as much of everything as he had. At the same time, though, Sabine recalls that Dietrich was a boy who was easily frightened so that she would, for example, follow behind him on his first walks to school in such a way as to allow him to appear independent while she provided accompaniment if necessary. Indeed, the story of the twins is one of a close and mutually supportive relationship, lasting throughout their lives, and one which we will have the opportunity to look at more closely later.

In broad outlines, the experiential structure of the Bonhoeffer children repeated the structure introduced by the parents, while adding to it a fullness that a large family can provide. The three older boys, as we have seen, were much like their father. The two who were permitted to live into adulthood both initiated successful academic and professional careers, and each—though particularly Karl-Friedrich—echoed their father's values. Likewise, each had little use for religion, an outlook they shared with their father. However, neither Karl-Friedrich nor Klaus was exactly like their father: Karl-Friedrich was heterodox enough to become a socialist, and Klaus did not share his father's even temper. The difference between them and their father was a difference of generations, and both Karl-Friedrich's politics and Klaus's hot temper probably can be attributed to their experiences in the First World War and related social and political events. What all this must have meant for Dietrich was that his masculine models were presented to him in at least two stages, adding a richness to his experience. Again, his sensitivity to a finely tuned notion of generations is reflected in his 1933 talk.

The same point can be made, though more forcefully, about the feminine models of Dietrich's childhood and youth. Ursula and Christine buffered his mother's influence undoubtedly in much the same way the three older boys did his father's. But, in addition to Ursula and Christine, there was his grandmother, Julie Bonhoeffer, who, as has been seen, Dietrich was quite fond of. At the same time, Dietrich's twin was a sister, and the third member of their family "cohort" was also a girl. Indeed, given the ages of the children, the fact that the Bonhoeffer household was a relatively self-contained social unit, and the fact that the rearing of the twins was placed in the hands of two governesses, the Horn sisters, it can be surmised that Dietrich was raised in a world of women—even if he had two-tiered male models to respect and emulate. What is more, this female world included not a few colorful people, most notably Paula Bonhoeffer.

The Family Context of Bonhoeffer's Life and Thought

The Bonhoeffers were an extremely close-knit family, so much so that even when grown the children continued to center their social and personal lives around the home of their parents. A glance at the map of key familial points in Berlin in 1943, provided by Bethge, reveals this strikingly.[15] All but two of the children, by then middle-aged with children of their own, lived in the same neighborhood as their parents. (Karl-Friedrich held a professorship at Leipzig and Sabine had been forced into a London exile.) Moreover, one surmises that the frequent evenings of music and discussion continued in the parents' home up until the time these occasions increasingly became evenings of conspiratorial discussion alone. Indeed, just days before Bonhoeffer's 1943 arrest, the entire family had gathered nervously to celebrate the senior Bonhoeffer's seventy-fifth birthday—nervously because, even though birthday wishes had been sent by Hitler himself, the family was awaiting the outcome of a coup. As this celebration illustrates, it was only on a profound pre-existing family solidarity that such a special kind of conspiratorial network could have arisen. The family was the social center of the Bonhoeffers' world, and it was because of this cohesiveness rather than the other way around that the Bonhoeffers could become a center of political resistance.

Although in some ways more independent than the others, especially in his pursuit of a theological career and in his intensely spiritual search, Dietrich was in other ways more closely allied with his family than were his brothers and sisters. Against a code of silence that one's personal affairs not be broadcast publicly, Emmi Bonhoeffer, a former neighbor who later married Klaus, asked a rather pointed question: had Paula Bonhoeffer spoiled Dietrich, who lived longer at home unmarried than the other children?[16] Even such a frank question implies an understatement. In fact, Dietrich was still living at home unmarried at the time of his arrest in 1943, when he was thirty-seven years old. To be sure, he had left home many times before: in 1923 he began his university studies at Tübingen; in 1924 he traveled to Rome and North Africa; in 1928 he was an assistant pastor in Barcelona; in 1930–31 he pursued postdoctoral studies at Union Theological Seminary in New York; in 1934–35 he took charge of parishes in London; in 1935–37 he lived with his seminarians at Finkenwalde; and from then on he lived only intermittently at his parents' home, traveling widely. These are, however, just qualifications. Only about seven of the twenty years between his seventeenth and thirty-seventh birthdays were actually spent by him in residences away from his parents. During the term at Tübingen he lived with his grandmother; the travels to Rome and North Africa were made in the company of his brother; the assistant pastorate in Barcelona was a requirement for ordination; and it is reported that while in London he telephoned home almost every night and visited frequently. Moreover, Bonhoeffer scholars have long since become familiar with their subject's complaints of homesickness whenever he was forced away from Berlin. And, finally, only once did Bonhoeffer move his personal library away from the family home, and that was to Finkenwalde, the one community outside of his family to which he was completely devoted. In short—except for Finkenwalde—it appears that Bonhoeffer not only lived longer at home than his siblings, but that he actually lived at home continuously except for short intervals until his imprisonment.

It is more difficult to speculate on Bonhoeffer's lifelong bachelorhood. The difficulty arises because, although it is reported that Bonhoeffer did have a girlfriend during his student years, the facts of the relationship (including the woman's identity) are carefully guarded by intimates. All we know is that she was a theology student, too, and that Bonhoeffer broke off the relationship sometime around 1935 in order to devote himself more single-mindedly to the Finkenwalde community. Then, eight years later, another young woman appeared in Bonhoeffer's life, one to whom he became engaged in 1943, but his imprisonment and later execution prevented their marrying. So, again, we find Emmi Bonhoeffer's question more than justified: Bonhoeffer in fact never married.

But the question posed by a social psychology of knowledge requires that we not only locate Bonhoeffer in a particular social context, but that we also consider the potential influences on his thought deriving from other contexts. For a theologian living during the Third Reich, the likely candidates for other contexts are his church, his country, and his teachers and colleagues. Now, we

have already seen that at least through the writing of his
dissertation—which of course is where he lays the foundation for
his lifelong commitment to sociality—Bonhoeffer rarely attended
church. Instead, religious services were typically held in the Bonhoeffer home, and only occasionally would Dietrich, usually
accompanied by his mother and maybe a sister, attend church
services. Sociologically, he simply could not have derived his
notion of sociality from the actual life of the church. Although it
is reported that Bonhoeffer was deeply impressed by the Catholic
church in Rome, here it suffices to say that a short visit somewhere
cannot constitute the context for a body of thought unless in that
visit is crystallized a host of pre-existing influences that somehow
come together there. Thus it is that the experience in Rome must
be understood as an occasion for integrating other, previous (and
later, insofar as the experience is remembered) experiences, and
it is the context of these other experiences that command the
attention of the social psychologist.

    In the previous chapter I already have had occasion to present
Bethge's evidence for the emergence of discipleship prior to the
rise of National Socialism; we need only be reminded of this here
to see that a political context is a difficult one in which to place
Bonhoeffer's thought about discipleship. To this should be added
two inferences about Bonhoeffer's political sensibilities. The first
is that all evidence indicates that prior to 1933 (when everyone
became conscious of politics) he was essentially naive and unin-
terested in politics, and even in the early years of the Nazi regime
he was strangely silent about the Nazi purges of the left. It appears,
then, that even as his political consciousness began to grow, he
invariably saw political issues through the lenses of church politics. This leads to the second inference. Between 1934 and 1935,
we have seen, Bonhoeffer was not even living in Germany but
had taken up pastorates in London, from where he nightly phoned
home. Very likely, it was in these telephone conversations (with

his mother in particular) that he kept abreast of the almost daily changes of events in the church struggle. Also, from letters in which he or his mother suggests certain theological books that might interest the other, we can infer that Paula Bonhoeffer kept up a fairly active program of theological reading alongside her son. (That his father did not is suggested not only by his father's agnosticism but also by the fact, which Bethge reports, that Bonhoeffer "rarely" tried to interest his father in a book he was reading.) In other words, we can surmise that even as Bonhoeffer began to learn about politics, it was largely in the context of his family that such learning occurred.

We come, then, to the question of Bonhoeffer's intellectual influences outside of his family. Surely no one could attend the University of Berlin in the 1920s (or Union Theological Seminary, for that matter) and remain uninfluenced by the scholarship of the day, and Bonhoeffer was indeed a learned man thoroughly acquainted with great ideas of his time and civilization. But where an attempt is made to trace these influences, especially in terms of specific teachers or intellectual traditions, the attempt reaches an impasse. The impasse is that Bonhoeffer, perhaps like other great thinkers wishing to preserve their intellectual independence as young persons, seemed almost purposely to avoid subordination to a mentor who would train him a bit too strongly in a school of thought that was not his. The one living theologian who exercised a profound influence on Bonhoeffer, for example, was Karl Barth. Both of Bonhoeffer's dissertations are heavily Barthian (much to the chagrin of the Berlin theologians), and yet Bonhoeffer resisted the temptation to study with Barth until July 1931, after postdoctoral studies in New York, when he attended a few of Barth's seminars in Bonn. Or, for another example, although a neighbor of the Bonhoeffers was the semiretired giant of church history, Adolf von Harnack, and although the younger man and the older man developed sufficient mutual liking for one another through neighborly and seminar contacts for Bonhoeffer to be asked to preach at Harnack's funeral, Bonhoeffer chose another theologian, Reinhold Seeberg, to lead him rather uneventfully through his studies. This is not to say that Seeberg contributed little to Bonhoeffer's training—Bethge reports that from Seeberg Bonhoeffer acquired an appreciation for the social and learned the rudiments of systematic theology—but, in comparison to Bonhoeffer's options, Seeberg was very likely chosen as a way of preserving intellectual independence rather than a way of apprenticeship. And, as might be imagined, the situation was more pronounced in New York, which left Bonhoeffer appalled at America's theological ignorance.

But there was a kind of influence to which Bonhoeffer was susceptible during his student years and throughout his life that was not limited to the immediate circle of the family: his friends. To be sure, in some ways this exception is the one that proves the rule, for, first, it is reported that Bonhoeffer did not make a true friend until he was twenty-one and met Franz Hildebrandt and, second, the friends he did make, like Hildebrandt and later Bethge, were invariably drawn into the Bonhoeffer family. Even Bethge, for example, observes that Bonhoeffer had a difficult time making friends and rarely had them in his school years, though he does not develop the point. Another recollection, this time by a fellow student in New York, recalls Bonhoeffer's aristocratic temperament that turned an invitation to a tennis match into a cold battle of egos.[17] Of the friends he did bring into the family, Hildebrandt considered the Bonhoeffers to be a "second home," while Bethge (whom Bonhoeffer did not meet until Finkenwalde) eventually married Bonhoeffer's niece. Moreover, because his friends were typically drawn from his juniors—Hildebrandt was younger and behind him in school; Bethge was his student; and even his fiancee was twenty years younger and a former pupil in his confirmation class—it was not intellectual companionship that he gained from them primarily, but something else.

What Bonhoeffer gained from his friendships can be illustrated by briefly considering three of them. First, Hildebrandt was a Jew, and it was in part his fight for Hildebrandt's right to hold a pastorate in Germany that Bonhoeffer became involved in the church struggle. (Later he helped Hildebrandt acquire a ministry in London.) Next, one of Bonhoeffer's American friends was Jean Lasserre, a Frenchman and a pacifist committed to the ecumenical movement. Upon arriving in the United States, Bonhoeffer had little use for either of these causes. After returning to Germany, it was the ecumenical movement in which Bonhoeffer had his most long-lived ecclesiastic career, and it was on pacifism that he meditated and talked, to the surprise of his German students. It was Lasserre, Bethge observes, who led Bonhoeffer to a new understanding of the Sermon on the Mount, the biblical basis for discipleship. Lastly, Bonhoeffer's friendship with Frank Fisher, a black American, appears to have been rather unstable, handicapped by the institutionalized racism of New York. But it was through Fisher that Bonhoeffer became acquainted with the Christian community in Harlem which he participated in, the Negro fiction which he absorbed, and the spirituals which he later taught his Finkenwalde students. Indeed, appalled by American theology and bored by mainstream American Protestantism, Bonhoeffer thought later it was the black church of Harlem which provided his most important lesson from America. At the time he wrote that the American race problem was even more severe than Germany's "Jewish question."

So Bonhoeffer did have influences outside the family. A powerful intellect, he had studied with some of the best minds of his generation—although he avoided subordination to them. He also let personal friendships—Hildebrandt, Lasserre, Fisher, perhaps his girlfriend—influence him profoundly. But these influences, it seems, were always sewn into the fabric of the context in which he lived as a child, a student, and an adult: his family.

Family, Sociality, and Polyphony

"Theology is an attempt," begins Dumas's theological interpretation of Bonhoeffer, "to speak about God in such a way that one is really speaking about *God*, and really *speaking* about him."[18] The best understanding that my layperson's theological sense can provide for a proposition like this one is that theology finds itself in a communicative quandary any time it postulates a truly absolute, authoritarian, and "radically other" God. That is, if God is really God—absolute and eternal—how can mere mortals really communicate with him? Conversely, if we can really communicate with God, is God really "above" us or, rather, are we not like gods as evidenced by our ability to have discourse with God? One way has God truly absolute—but beyond our reach; the other way has God within our reach—but not truly absolute. As I understand the matter, this is something of a perennial paradox in theology, and one that was particularly pressing in 1921 when the second edition of Karl Barth's *Epistle to the Romans* appeared.[19]

Barth and the "dialectical," "crisis," or "neo-orthodox" theology, which his approach is variously named, shook the theological world with the assertion—contrary to the prevailing school of liberal theology that had its heyday in nineteenth-century and early-twentieth-century Germany—that the Word of God, though it does in fact reach man, is launched from a reach beyond man and is incomprehensible to man in any mode other than receptivity. Put another way, Barth insisted that God speaks to humankind from a position of absolute advantage, and humankind deludes itself when it supposes it can speak in return to God unless it does so by the sheer grace of God, whose prior Word to humankind provides the channel of response that humankind can take. This orientation (for it is really more than an idea) is what Bonhoeffer accepted in his student years and, on the whole, never wavered from afterwards. But from the start Bonhoeffer supplemented this orientation with a sociological understanding of humankind that anchored the free and absolute Word in the concrete human community. This, again, was Bonhoeffer's great modification of and contribution to Barth's orientation, though Bonhoeffer himself always considered his position to be fully in the middle of both the Barthian and liberal schools, rather than subordinate to either. That is, from *The Communion of Saints* through *Letters and Papers from Prison* Bonhoeffer's self-conception was that, as a theologian, his distinctive position was that of straddling the new Barthian theology and the liberal theology of his training and heritage.

Families, too, must wrestle with the tension between authority and sociality. The family, after all, is the paradigmatic instance of a social group in which power differentials are ubiquitous and natural—no infant could be granted the same social power as an adult. But the family is also the paradigmatic instance of a social group in which a premium is placed on the values of love, solidarity, and individual expression. In cases like Bonhoeffer's, where family ties are especially strong, the family must therefore be considered as a kind of pre-ethical prototype for working out the relationship between power and sociality. The ethical sense of a family is that which, were it full blown, would be considered a theory of justice, in that it legitimates power, translating it into authority, but it does so in such a way that the values of sociality are still affirmed.

Returning to the quotation from *The Communion of Saints* with which this chapter was begun, we are now in a better position to appreciate the relationship between the structure of Bonhoeffer's family and the structure of his thought. Bonhoeffer has been shown to have been immersed in a close-knit family headed by an authoritarian, if humanitarian, patriarch. But he also was allied especially with his mother in this family: his closest siblings by order of birth were girls, he was perhaps "spoiled" by his mother, and he embraced the religiosity that was an aspect of his mother's rather than his father's world. Thus, in *The Communion of Saints* we see Bonhoeffer's (Barthian) presupposition about the absolute and unquestioned authority of the Word of God (and the patriarch in the family), together with his almost compulsive unconcern with defending this presupposition and his equally compulsive orientation toward serving and preserving the community which is headed by the patriarch. In a passage that illustrates this outlook and also anticipates the tension in his views that will later explode in political action, he writes in that same book: "The transcendence of the Thou has nothing to do with epistemological transcendence. This is a purely moral transcendence, which is experienced only by the man who makes a decision, which can never be demonstrated to someone standing outside."[20] The important point here is how Bonhoeffer places himself inside the community in which moral transcendence makes sense—inside his actual family and allied with his mother, and inside the church in which the Word is received. Also noteworthy, however, is the idea that transcendence is achieved within the community simply by making a decision, or through "responsible action" as he sometimes puts it in his writings. For one day, a day when Bonhoeffer severs his exclusive alliance with his mother and joins forces with his father and brothers in political conspiracy, it is only with the idea of responsible action, of a decision from within a milieu where that decision makes sense, that Bonhoeffer will come close to justifying his actions to himself. But in the beginning, in his dissertation, he simply sketches the foundation for that potentiality and, for the

most part, strives to serve the community beneath an unquestioned authority of another.

In this discussion we will be able to deepen our understanding
of the conflictual elements of Bonhoeffer's attempt to hold fast to
the absolute deference to God and the commitment to sociality.
In political and religious terms, the conflict is met when solidarity
with humanity demands disobedience to governmental institutions to which God demands obedience. But in familial terms the
conflict will be seen much more quickly in the submerged but
real conflict between Paula and Karl Bonhoeffer on matters of
faith. It is this conflict that is drilled into the psychological constitution of Dietrich long before it is writ large in the political
arena.

The conflict and its resolution are apparent throughout Bonhoeffer's intellectual career. Even in his dissertation, despite its
Barth-proclaimed status as a "theological miracle," the conflict
emerges in the tension between the spoken commitment to the
concrete, actual Christian community and the abstract, formalistic,
and reified sociological constructs used to define that community.[21] The sociality Bonhoeffer celebrates in his dissertation is, in
the final analysis, a conceptual rather than a real sociality, an
existential mistake that is hinted at by the overly abstract, turgid
style of the piece. Indeed, Bonhoeffer's above-quoted assertion
that transcendence does not mean epistemological transcendence
serves both to distinguish his position from Kantianism and to
preserve an intellectual space for himself to write authoritatively
about things that, according to his own argument, cannot be pronounced authoritatively from the outside. To be sure, there is
probably more than a tension in *The Communion of Saints*; there
is probably rather an out-and-out contradiction above which the
thesis cannot rise. And this is why the book has been little read
and rarely heralded as anything more than a good exercise by a
theologian who would later become great. What is important about

The Communion of Saints, for present purposes as well as for theological and sociological purposes generally, then, is that it represents an ambitious, albeit unsuccessful, attempt of a man to think of the Christian faith as an inherently social enterprise.

The attempt and the tension continue. In his 1933 lectures on christology at the University of Berlin, for example, Bonhoeffer struggles in even more cumbersome verbal formulation to express the union of immanence and transcendence. There he tries to explain that "Christ is at one and the same time, my boundary and my rediscovered centre. He is the centre, between 'I' and 'I,' and between 'I' and God. The boundary can only be known as a boundary from beyond the boundary. In Christ, man recognizes it and thereby at the same time finds his new centre again."[22] This formulation is of almost impenetrable obscurity. Later, in *Letters and Papers from Prison*, the same idea is expressed a little more clearly. There he writes: "I should like to speak of God not on the boundaries but at the centre, not in weakness but in strength; and therefore not in death and guilt but in man's life and goodness. . . . God's 'beyond' is not the beyond of our cognitive faculties. The transcendence of epistemological theory has nothing to do with the transcendence of God. God is beyond in the midst of our life."[23] Thus, the conflict which is here being traced is one that follows Bonhoeffer into his final years as well as one that appears in his first theological work. The substance of the conflict is the effort to both speak about *God* and *speak* about him, as Dumas put it. It is a conflict that Bonhoeffer strives to resolve sociologically and by a commitment to sociality. And because his sociological solution is ultimately unsuccessful—that is, the intellectual argument alone does not suffice—the contradiction is chiseled into an ethic where it lives as an existential paradox. But, finally, the conflict is rooted in another sociopsychological conflict—that between Bonhoeffer's devout mother, with whom he was allied, and his agnostic patriarchal father, whom he obeyed.

Reconciling the two is sociality—the task that was on the whole accomplished so well in his large and diverse yet extremely close-knit family—was the leitmotif of his life and thought, which the ethic of discipleship epitomizes.

But the ultimate ambition of this study is larger than simply tracing Bonhoeffer's ethic of discipleship to the family milieu in which it was shaped; my ultimate purpose is to show how through discipleship Bonhoeffer enacted a lifelong struggle that led him finally to personal liberation. It is therefore interesting to observe that very late in his life Bonhoeffer hit upon another metaphor to express the paradox that he had before tried to express in the clumsy spatial metaphors of "beyond" and "within" and so forth. That metaphor was a musical one, and when he hit upon it he expressed great "joy," for it expressed better than anything else the simultaneous commitment to a God who is "wholly other" and yet the social world in which his Word is embedded. The metaphor is polyphony, a fugue in which a primary and unchanging melody (the *cantus firmus*) is progressively joined by counterpointed melodies which superficially oppose it but, taken as a whole, blend together into a powerful harmonic whole. What Bonhoeffer liked about it was the way in which the metaphor expressed the "multi-dimensionality" of the Christian life. Here is how he put it less than eleven months before his execution: "God wants us to love him eternally and with our whole hearts—not in such a way to injure or weaken our earthly love, but to provide a kind of *cantus firmus* to which the other melodies of life provide the counterpoint. . . . Only a polyphony of this kind can give life a wholeness and at the same time assure us that nothing calamitous can happen so long as the *cantus firmus* is kept going."[24] Clearly this metaphor of polyphony does express the paradox between authoritarian subordination and sociality better than do the spatial metaphors. Clearly, too, it captures nicely the paradox of the disciple whose commitment to humanity led to his imprisonment and execution by a totalitarian political regime. Finally, it is also clear that polyphony is a good way to express the harmony found in a family with strong and diverse personalities yet a powerful sense of solidarity. What is especially interesting here is that in the final months of his life, when Bonhoeffer had traveled the path of discipleship through its negation and therefore to its psychological fulfillment, the freed Bonhoeffer discovered a metaphor rooted even earlier in his life than was theology, for before he became a theologian Bonhoeffer had been a pianist. Only in the final months of his life was he able to re-experience these earliest harmonic beginnings drawn from a time before the family crisis led him to embark upon a path as a theologian and ethicist.

A certain sense of Bonhoeffer's unique position in his family can be gleaned by reconsidering a scene with which we already have become acquainted. The scene epitomizes the sociality which was so characteristic of the Bonhoeffer family and to which Dietrich Bonhoeffer was committed in his thought and practice. It is the scene of the family parties where parents, children, and their spouses and friends would gather in the Bonhoeffer home for an evening of music and conversation. Yet something peculiar about Dietrich's behavior during them is almost universally recalled by his intimates: that in the midst of the festivities Dietrich would often slip away to go to his room alone. With the exception, perhaps, of his fiancée, Maria von Wedemeyer, no one ever asked him why he did this, and he never explained it to his family.[25] Bethge, who joined Bonhoeffer in the practice of mutual confession and so may know, simply reports that because Bonhoeffer was lonely he became a theologian, and because he was a theologian he was lonely. This cryptic explanation reveals more than it appears to. On one hand, the aura of loneliness, sadness, and isolation surrounding Bonhoeffer was a psychological characteristic of his recognized by many. On the other hand, the genesis of this aura is somehow related to his vocation as a theologian. In the next chapter, I will trace the forces which led Bonhoeffer to emerge from a polyphonic beginning with a commitment to sociality to accept a posture of isolation, a development that led him to become a theologian and an ethicist.

IIII

The Making of a
Theologian and an Ethicist

"There was something that united us, something that we owed our parents," observed Bonhoeffer's twin sister years later in her book-length "portrait" of her family.[1] The remark is worth savoring, particularly when it is compared to Bethge's observation that Bonhoeffer grew up in "a family that derived its real education, not from school, but from a deeply-rooted sense of being guardians to a great historical heritage and intellectual tradition."[2] For Bethge's observation sketches the contours of history and heritage to which Bonhoeffer felt an obligation via the mediation of his family that had handed these gifts on to him. But Sabine's remark suggests that there was also an inner dimension to this diffuse sense of obligation felt by the Bonhoeffers: there was "something"—she writes, without being quite able to articulate that "something"—that the Bonhoeffer children owed specifically to their parents. Indeed, this "something" grows increasingly large when we recall that a sense of obligation led the Bonhoeffer children into a political resistance that would cost many of them their lives, even though none was personally threatened by the Reich. "Something" led them into calamitous actions, and this "something" was also the stuff that held their family together, if again we can appreciate Sabine's comment in its fullest implications. My thesis is that once this "something" is uncovered we will also discover the motives for Dietrich's decision to become a theologian and, in particular, the sociopsychological constellation out of which emerged the paradox of costly grace.

The road we are on is one of psychological biography and so has its theoretical dimensions. To reiterate, I am assuming that the ubiquitous power differences in families, combined with each family's commitment to solidarity, lead families to erect an ethos which legitimates power at the same time that it preserves solidarity. The ethos is essential, and it is nothing less than the family's private ethical code and theory of justice. Now, when injustice encroaches upon the family, particularly the parental generation, the family ethos takes as its task the rectification of this injustice in some envisioned future. Not surprisingly, it is typically the children who are asked to play the major role in rectifying this injustice insofar as their relative youth induces the parents to look to them as human embodiment of their hopes for a more just future. This process is theorized to occur in all families, though where family solidarity and authority are particularly strong, or injustice is particularly keen, the process would be more intense than in other cases. In the case of the Bonhoeffers, who evidenced strong authoritarianism and solidarity—as shown by many indicators, but especially their political resistance—it is likely that we

will find an equally intense family ethos and a terribly keen perception of family injustice. And, in any family that produces an
ethicist, it must be hypothesized that his role in the creation and
unfolding of the family scenario is a quite specific one. This is
what will be shown about Dietrich Bonhoeffer: how a specific
constellation of familial events surrounding a specific family injustice predestined his choice of career and colored a large part of
its character.

The aspect of Bonhoeffer's thought to which I think the events
to be described in this chapter are most influential is his notion
of costly grace, which inaugurates through metaphor his ethic of
discipleship. Recalling my previous discussion of this paradox of
discipleship, the reader will remember my suggestion that within
the metaphor of costly grace actually lurked two distinct paradoxes: that the "cost" of grace is the absolute cost of death, and
that the idea of grace having a "cost" is a metaphor erected only
to be shattered and so to show the paradox of trying to apply
human reasoning to spiritual realities. In the main, this chapter
addresses only the first of these paradoxes, death as the cost of
grace. To anticipate, I will argue quite directly that it was the death
of Bonhoeffer's brother in 1918, and the family trauma surrounding it, that induced Dietrich to become a theologian and ethicist.
But I also want in this chapter to suggest a linkage between the
existential paradox of death as the cost of grace and the purely
intellectual paradox of the cost of grace as being incalculable. This
linkage, moreover, will also highlight the relationship between
Bonhoeffer's notion of costly grace and his commitment to sociality. Since these linkages are subtle ones and their articulation
is submerged in this chapter beneath the main interpretation of
death as an impetus to discipleship, let me briefly explain what I
think these linkages are.

At issue is the philosophical question of the relationship between
human reason and human ends. After all, the second paradox of

costly grace is nothing other than a critique of human reason—or a certain mode of human reason in the point to be developed here—when applied to spiritual ends. To understand this issue, let us join other scholars in returning to Aristotle. According to Aristotle, there are three relatively distinct types of human rationality. These are the productive, the practical, and the theoretical. Productive rationality is a calculative, means-ends mode of reasoning which humankind applies to the world of nature to wrest its sustenance for living. Theoretical rationality is the reasoning process applied to the problems of ontology—physics and "first philosophy" were Aristotle's examples, though we might say simply pure science. Between these two modes of rationality is practical rationality, by which Aristotle meant reason applied to the affairs of the human community, be it in the ethical domain of, say, friendship, or in the domain of the polis. One way to grasp the distinction among these types of rationality is through a temporal dimension. For Aristotle, theoretical reason is applied to the permanent and eternal, productive reason to the constantly changing and cyclical requirements for physical survival, and practical reason to the *relatively permanent* domain of the human community, which is greater than the individual, as is shown by its outliving the individual, but is not eternal.

The point of these distinctions for modern political discourse is to raise the question of whether or not modern civilization applies the appropriate mode of rationality to the proper arena. The contemporary argument—one which, interestingly, was anticipated by Bonhoeffer (as will be discussed in Chapter V)—is that the contemporary west has subordinated both theoretical and practical rationality to productive rationality. This downgrading happened because, under capitalism, science (theoretical rationality) came to be a tool only for capitalism's technological advancement, and so was robbed of its inherent teleology, the contemplation of truth as such. Modern scientific technology is

in fact but highly sophisticated productive rationality. But, con-
comitantly, the rise of the social sciences was also coopted by
capitalist culture along with the natural sciences, so that even the
study of human social and political life is now viewed as a "technical" problem of human "engineering." The result is that the
western mind now implicitly thinks only in a productive mode,
even when it seeks to apply reason to problems of ontology and
politics. Thus there has emerged a critique of instrumental or
technical reason as the premise for critical reflection in either
politics or religion. To be sure, critical views are often associated
with the neo-Marxian perspective of the critical theorists, but it is
worth noting that religious thinkers like Paul Tillich and Jacques
Ellul present similar views.[3] Moreover, I am suggesting that Bonhoeffer, too, presented such a critique.

The second paradox of costly grace—which in effect is set up
only to destroy the possibility of using (quantitative) human rationality to fathom the depths of grace—is most fundamentally a critique of instrumental reason and a search for another mode of
rationality by which grace can be grasped. And the other mode
of rationality for which Bonhoeffer clearly searches is what Aristotle dubbed the "practical" mode. It is an inherently social mode
of reason, and that which Bonhoeffer began to erect in his dissertation and continued to defend throughout his life. Thus, the
second paradox of costly grace is intimately related to the paradox
of sociality, for the critique of instrumental reason is also a cry
for a practical, social mode of rationality which should take its
place. In this way, the present explication of the paradox of costly
grace represents a continuity with my previous explication of the
paradox of sociality. I will make this plain in the course of the
interpretation by linking what is discovered about costly grace to
Bonhoeffer's commitment to sociality.

Only one question remains. It is how to relate the two paradoxes of costly grace, death, and the critique of instrumental

reason. This linkage is discovered sociopsychologically, though it can also be asserted theoretically. Of importance sociopsychologically is the fact that the death to which I will trace Bonhoeffer's ethical impetus was not an isolated event but an event in a social context. That is, I will show that the significance of his brother's death to Bonhoeffer was not so much the event itself as it was the family's *reaction* to the event. Thus, if the fact of death constitutes one of the paradoxes nestled within costly grace, the family events surrounding a son's death raise the problem of the other paradox of costly grace: the appropriate mode of rationality to apply both to the ultimate questions of religious truth and to the practical questions of preserving a (family) community that is threatened with dissolution in the face of death. In this way, although the paradoxes may be analytically distinguished, they are also shown to be cemented together in a moral mosaic which, ultimately, enables discipleship to cohere as a unitary ethic. Questions of death, sociality, and the critique of instrumental reason are intimately blended in the ethic of discipleship, as they also were fused in the experiences of a boy whose family home came to near collapse when the news that his brother had died reached his parents in April 1918. The circumstance that it was a wartime death, combined with the Bonhoeffers' pre-existing distaste for the military, readied the Bonhoeffers for action when, fifteen years later, a similar calamity threatened to befall the nation of which they considered themselves historical and intellectual guardians.

To be prepared for the biographical interpretation that follows, one needs most to recall the general influence of Paula Bonhoeffer over her son's earliest religious life, for it is their relationship that is central for understanding the facts that follow. To elaborate briefly, Paula Bonhoeffer was a peculiarly devout woman who as a girl had adopted the ideals of the Moravian Brethren with what Bethge calls "youthful enthusiasm" and whose lineage included not a few clergymen. And even if she kept her religiosity "below the surface" after her marriage to Karl Bonhoeffer, she did take personal charge of her children's religious education and employed a genuine follower of the Moravian Brethren, Maria Horn, as governess for the twins.

By contrast, though Karl Bonhoeffer would attend the family religious gatherings, "setting an example of how the feelings of others should be shared and respected," it was still the case that "everyone knew that this was their mother's affair."[4] Indeed, about his wife's piety Karl Bonhoeffer would say "I understand nothing of that" in what Bethge calls a "tone of condescending humour," tempered by only a "trace" of respect for the inadequacies of human reason.[5] And, because of his son's decision to pursue a career in the church, Karl Bonhoeffer "pitied" him and later told him so.[6] In short, if the son's act was in part a critique of his father and the instrumental rationality he epitomized in his positivistic and agnostic temperament, it was in larger part through an alliance with his mother that Dietrich first became a Christian and an ethicist. My hunch here is that what Dietrich "owed" his parents was primarily owed to his mother, so it is a family scene in which they are the principal actors where we shall likely find the generation of forces that catapulted Dietrich into theology and ethics. Interestingly, this is the scene the mature theologian presents to us, only thinly veiled, in the fictional writings that occupied his time during his first year of imprisonment—very likely the soliloquies that served to sever finally the bonds of the family events that had held him psychologically imprisoned for some twenty-five years.

An Allegory of Death

Bonhoeffer's prison fiction deals almost exclusively with family themes. He himself wrote that "there is a good deal of autobiography mixed up in it";[7] Zerner argues that it reflects a quest for self-discovery;[8] and Green comments that it "is not fiction in the sense of pure imaginative construct, but rather autobiography and social memory expressed by imagination in the *form* of . . . fiction."[9] Now, within these writings is a story—a kind of allegory—which recurs in a novel fragment after having been used in a slightly different version for the opening of a drama. This repetition alone suggests its significance. It is a story, based loosely on an event from family history, which Bonhoeffer uses to set the stage for what he wants to say (and discover) about his family. Its theme is death, and here is how he presents it, the second time, in his novel fragment:

> A shrill scream made her jump. She recognized Little Brother's voice; the child wasn't visible. It wasn't usually his way to cry even when he was hurt. And it sounded less a cry for help than one of rage. Frau Brake was already on the steps to the garden and hurried toward the wilderness without being able to spot Little Brother. Then she heard soft weeping and found the boys kneeling in the bushes. Little Brother was holding a young bird.
>
> "She pushed it out of the nest," he said, tears streaming down his face, when he saw the grandmother.
>
> "Who, the cat again?"
>
> "No, much worse; the mother herself, the bad, mean beast."
>
> The young bird twitched once more and then died in the boy's hand. That was too much for him. Frightened, he involuntarily opened his hand and dropped the dead little robin. Then he felt shame, reached again for the little bird, stood up, and showed it to his grandmother.[10]

For purposes of comparison, let us note the actual incident upon which this allegory is based. Karl Bonhoeffer noted it in his memoirs:

> In our little summer house in the Harz Mountains, he
> was usually in the woods at sunrise. He knew all the birds
> and was able to call them. A passionate hunter, he made
> friends with the foresters wherever he was and early on
> became an excellent shot. I witnessed him shooting a
> circling falcon. But when the bird fell down dead in front
> of him he was so shaken that he burst into tears.[11]

Proof that this is the incident is that, when the allegory first appears, the animal dies after being shot by a hunter. It follows that the reason for the modification of the story in its second version, quoted above, is that this version is designed to portray more of the psychological, if less of the historical, "truth" of the incident.

The theme of the allegory is, obviously, the senselessness of death. But a look now at some of the more subtle dimensions of this literary construct will allow us to build a bridge between the influence of Bonhoeffer's mother on him and this theme of death in his thought (and political action). There are two such observations of particular merit.

First, we note with some interest that the editors of *Fiction from Prison* claim that the "Little Brother" character is based, in large part, on Bonhoeffer himself. Thus, we see what role Bonhoeffer assigned himself in the allegory: the boy who witnesses and is shamed by the ordeal. Yet—and this is the crucial point— the actual event upon which the story is based, that event "witnessed" by Karl Bonhoeffer, did not involve Dietrich at all. Instead, the person Karl Bonhoeffer writes about is *Walter* Bonhoeffer, the son who died of wounds received in the First World War; it was he who was the actor in the real-life event. Indeed, as though to reveal further that he is speaking of his brother Walter, the bird in the allegory is both young—as Little Brother is and as was Walter when he died—and does not die immediately as it had in the actual event but dies later, as did Walter. But, most important, this story about Walter is appropriated to the author himself, and we see Bonhoeffer both "witnessing" the event (which he probably had not in real life) and identifying with the dead bird/ brother, an impossible feat in life but one possible both psychologically and in literature. Hence, we should prepare ourselves to see in Bonhoeffer's youth a propensity both to identify with Walter and a compulsion to witness his death as a shamed younger brother and, perhaps, moral commentator—his role as author of the allegory.

The second feature of this allegory that is of seemingly crucial psychological interest is that, whereas in the actual event and the first version of the story it is a hunter who is responsible for the bird's death, in this version it is the mother herself who causes the young bird to die. She pushes it out of the nest, allowing it to fall to a slow death. Could this be a veiled accusation by Bonhoeffer that his mother was, in part, guilty of Walter's death? Whereas this is a stronger inference than is warranted by the allegory itself, it does seem that the guilty party in the story is the mother—though her guilt is subsumed under the dictates of nature. Indeed, two additional points in the story contribute to the plausibility of this interpretation. First, it should be noted that, whereas the young bird and Little Brother parallel one another in the story, the mother of the bird finds no human counterpart. Instead, and almost as though through embarrassment in bringing the human mother into the story for fear of what it would reveal, Bonhoeffer constructs a human maternal figure in the grandmother, a character the editors say is modeled after Julie Bonhoeffer. It appears, then, that Bonhoeffer was aware at some level that his allegory implied a certain condemnation of his mother; in order to prevent these feelings from becoming too potent, he left the human mother out of the story and substituted for her a grandmother who could play the maternal role without having to take on its guilt. Thus, the very absence of the human mother in the allegory suggests that, indeed, the story involved a painful indictment of her. And the second clue making this assumption of the real mother's guilt plausible is that, toward the end of the story, Little Brother feels shame for *dropping the "dead little robin."* Note that the story ties this feeling of shame with the dropping of the bird, which, of course, is what the bird's mother had done to cause its death. The shame, then, structurally parallels the guilt here being attributed to the mother, and so it again suggests a feeling of Bonhoeffer's that his mother was guilty over the death of Walter—a feeling that produced shame in him.

What this story points to, therefore, is the impact that Walter's death had on the Bonhoeffer family and, in particular, on the relationship between son Dietrich and his mother. Indeed, I intend to argue that it was the event of this death and the reactions to it in the Bonhoeffer family that instilled in Dietrich, age twelve at the time, the motivation for becoming a theologian and an ethicist. Moreover, my argument will be that it is this familial complex which accounts, in large part, for the character of his thought and action. These suppositions find their first and most general validation in the fact that when Bonhoeffer delved into the roots of his faith during his first year of imprisonment, he chose to write and rewrite an allegory of the event of his brother's death.

Reactions to Walter's Death

The Bonhoeffer children were no strangers to death. In the year that Dietrich and Sabine were born a cousin, Wolf, Count von Kalckreuth, committed suicide. A portrait of this cousin hung in the Friedrichsbrunn home, and the children are said to have been preoccupied with the riddle of his suicide. Then, of course, came the war, and news of the deaths of friends and neighbors became commonplace. But it was not until 28 April 1918 that death entered the nuclear Bonhoeffer family. That was the day on which Walter Bonhoeffer died of wounds received in the war. Dietrich was twelve when the news came.

The death of their brother had a profound impact on the Bonhoeffer children. Christine, who was especially close to Walter, is reported to have "lost her childhood world."[12] Klaus and Ursula both named sons Walter, and Sabine reports having prayed for nearly a year that the body the family had buried had not been Walter's. As for Dietrich, it is reported that he is the one who played the farewell piece for Walter on the day of his departure and that, after his death, he and Sabine began a program of meditation on death and eternity. More will be said about this meditation below.

But it was not the children who appear to have been most devastated by the news of Walter's death; rather, it was the parents. When Sabine remembers praying that the buried body was not Walter's, for example, she adds to her recollection that it was not so much out of her own grief that she prayed, but because it seemed to her to be "the only way of bringing back any happiness to my parents."[13] Indeed, Karl and Paula Bonhoeffer both were shattered by the news of their son's death. Karl Bonhoeffer, for example, broke off keeping the family memoirs for ten long years following 1918, although he had kept them "punctiliously" up until then. It appears that in the aftermath of Walter's death this "remote and reserved" patriarch harbored too much pain to be able to chronicle the events of a family without its second son. And, by all accounts, Paula Bonhoeffer fared even worse. Bethge says that she "seemed broken" and that it was "a long time" before she recovered,[14] and Sabine echoes this account, adding to it that she recovered only through "her faith and the loving care of our father."[15] But, however accurate this may be, the fact is that Paula Bonhoeffer did not even recover at home; instead, "she spent weeks in bed at their next-door neighbors'."[16] She appears, then, to have barely made it through the ordeal. And, as for the impact of Walter's death on the parents jointly, it is remembered that on the day the telegram arrived, the two went upstairs not to come down again until the following day.

Now, beyond this description of the family's reaction to Walter's death the biographical sources do not go. Even so, the inference can be made that this relative silence is but an echo of the silence that the Bonhoeffers endured following 1918. What little is reported speaks volumes about the pain that this event produced, and it is not surprising that good taste and respect for the feelings of the living would deter biographers from dwelling on this event and its aftermath. Yet, the point to be made here is that Walter's death was a major tragedy for the Bonhoeffer family: Karl Bonhoeffer could not be said to have fully recovered for a decade, and, for some undetermined period that biographers simply say was "a long time," we know that the psychological state of Paula Bonhoeffer teetered precariously close to illness.

What I want to postulate here, then, is that Walter's death found the Bonhoeffer family at its most vulnerable point internally: the point at which its solidarity was most threatened. The argument follows that it was in response to this event that the Bonhoeffers invoked their deepest layers of family justice—just as, from a familial perspective, the death of Walter was the most unjust event to happen to the family. Now, lest this argument be pushed into foolishness, I am not supposing that it was only in reaction to this event that a sense of family justice emerged. Rather, the supposition is that the event of Walter's death gave the family an opportunity—indeed, compelled them—to intensify an existing ethos so as to enable them to handle this most crucial and threatening phase of their domestic lives. This response, in my view, is the significance of this event for the present interpretation: it throws into relief existing familial values and aspirations while at the same time it intensifies them.

Specifically, a kind of family "bargain" seems to have been struck between the religious and irreligious factions—that is, between the mother and the father. This "bargain" was to be a kind of solution to the pain of Walter's death. Its substance was that young Dietrich would be allowed to continue his religious pursuits and so to offer himself to his mother as a kind of replacement for Walter while, at the same time, possibly overcoming the limitations of Walter's memory by engaging in the one endeavor which promised a way out of death: religion. Karl Bonhoeffer, himself struck down by the senselessness of his son's death, would agree to look the other way as Dietrich and Paula formed a religious alliance. And Paul Bonhoeffer, overcome by an undeserved though understandable mother's guilt over Walter's death, would maintain over Dietrich the kind of influence she had relinquished with her elder sons.

But why should Paula Bonhoeffer have felt guilty over the death of her son when it was in no way her fault? Indeed, in the prison fiction just examined we found guilt attributed to the maternal figures, experienced as shame by Little Brother/Dietrich. Moreover, theoretically, were it not for the existence of psychological guilt over Walter's death, the motives that led to the family bargain hypothesized here would hardly have existed, for the bonds of social obligation are psychologically the chains of guilt. And, were it not for the internalization of the parental guilt by Dietrich, he would neither have adopted his familial "script" nor displayed the ambivalence toward it (and his mother) that we see in his fiction, where he vacillates between acceptance of his role and shame and rage in the face of the events that created it for him.

For the most part we must be content to witness the facts of guilt even if their explanation eludes us. But we might speculate along one or another lines. For one, because Walter did not die immediately but after a stay in a military hospital, and because Karl Bonhoeffer was a physician, the parents might have felt guilt over not having done more to ensure their son's recovery.[17] If this hypothesis is true, it would suggest that the guilt would have been experienced primarily by Karl Bonhoeffer—and that what we see as guilt in Paula Bonhoeffer was, in fact, misdirected rage at her husband. To be sure, this speculation fits with the facts that Walter, the Bonhoeffers' second son and a rather frail and sensitive boy also, was considered to be more like his mother than his father, and so was likely tacitly understood to be her special son. If so, the mere suspicion of paternal neglect leading to his death would have enraged Paula Bonhoeffer and so recalled and intensified the cleavage that already existed "beneath the surface" between them. Why this rage might have been internalized as guilt by Paula Bonhoeffer can probably be explained by the process of "identification with the oppressor," which has long been understood as a fairly common sociopsychological posture of the subordinate, though it has only recently been understood to be a frequent "ploy" of wives who suffer subordination and sometimes abuse at the hands of patriarchal husbands. Furthermore, if such a process did occur, it would account for the fact that Paula Bonhoeffer chose to spend her period of recuperation away from the family, since her initial reaction must have been rage rather than guilt. Finally, if this hypothesized explanation is substantially correct, it bespeaks a fundamental irrationality that is itself revealing. For, as a matter of fact, Karl Bonhoeffer probably could not have done anything to prevent Walter's death, and the perception that he thought he could suggests an inflated conception of his importance. This, too, might have enraged Paula Bonhoeffer, who all along had a lower opinion of a scientifically inclined intellect that could produce only agnosticism in the face of life's most crucial challenges. In any event, some such explanation seems plausible because it would account for the appearance of guilt in the family experience as well as the intensified cleavage between Paula and Karl Bonhoeffer, and between religion and science in the mind

of Dietrich. Then, too, such an explanation enables us to appreciate the mixture of guilt and rage which caused Dietrich at once
to identify with Walter and to take up the challenge posed by his
death, and yet also to feel sufficient shame over his mother's
behavior to omit her from direct reference in his prison fiction.
This shame would be rage reworked after his identification with
the family; it would be rage from the perspective of an insider.
After all, Dietrich had a right to be enraged at his parents, particularly his mother, who used him as a human tool to effect a family
bargain. Yet, because he accepted the task, his rage would have
to be submerged and translated into guilt and shame.

Of course, all of this is speculation. Alternatively, it could be
asserted, simply, that guilt is a natural, if irrational, reaction of
those who suffer the loss of a loved one. Parents, in particular,
who have made it their responsibility to ensure the safety of their
children, would quite naturally be susceptible to guilt when faced
with the death of a child, even though their guilt might be baseless.
It would simply flow from the general sense of obligation that
good parents everywhere feel for their children. And, to be sure,
this explanation adds to the sociopsychological richness of the
general interpretation of Bonhoeffer advanced here, but this
enrichment is not a sufficient reason to consider it true. Rather,
we are well on our way if only the fact of guilt is recognized,
whatever the cause.

Let us therefore backtrack for a moment in order to appreciate
how the coalescing of several chance events made the "bargain"
we are considering a quite natural affair. First, it will be remembered that Dietrich and his mother were already quite close and
that the mother had already instilled in her youngest children the
rudiments of her faith. Second, it will also be remembered that
Dietrich was what his twin sister termed a "chivalrous" boy, sensitive to others' pain and disposed to assist if there was any way
that he could. This would have predisposed him to consent to a
helpful parental "bargain." Third, it should be noted that the events

of concern were unfolding in the year or so following Dietrich's twelfth birthday, that this was just about the age that a Bonhoeffer male would choose an occupation, that his two elder brothers were already committed to their future professions, and that Dietrich was the only male child remaining for the parents to "choose" from if they wanted something different or special in a son—in short, Dietrich was *available*. Bethge has mentioned that there was an inclination, at least so far as Karl-Friedrich and Klaus were concerned, to look to Dietrich as a kind of replacement for Walter. All that is being supposed here is that this inclination was shared— in part, no doubt, despite themselves—by his parents. And, in practice, what this amounted to was but an intensification of an existing loyalty between mother and son on things Christian.

Just as Walter's death did not so much *cause* Dietrich to decide on a career in theology but, rather, intensified an existing tendency and fleshed it out with fairly specific familial obligations, so also there is an indicator of this family's bargain which is not as important in itself as it is for what is symbolizes. This is that Dietrich was given as a gift the bible that had belonged to Walter.[18] The giving of such a gift undoubtedly has elements of a parental injunction: that through his faith, Dietrich would somehow be able to "make up" for Walter's death and the parental guilt surrounding it. But for such a gift to have its desired effect, of course, it must be received in something close to the spirit in which it was given. This it most surely was, for it was Walter's bible that Bonhoeffer used for his personal meditations throughout his life. In all—for he also wore a ring bearing the Bonhoeffer coat of arms— Bonhoeffer's religious pilgrimage appears to have been firmly anchored in the spirit of his family, and this spirit reached its sharpest focus when Walter died and Dietrich was choosing his vocation.

But thus far we have only described the reactions of the Bonhoeffer family to the death of their son and argued from it that they would look to Dietrich as a kind of religious answer to their loss and grief. We have not yet, however, looked at Dietrich's experiences during this period—or examined to what, indeed, he attributed his choice of vocation.

Death and the Call to Christ

As a boy, Bonhoeffer displayed enough talent in music to make his family suppose that he would follow it as a career. Why he did not, and why he announced at age fourteen that he would study theology instead of music, is what must be discussed here. The answer to this question, crystallized in the recollection that it was Dietrich who played the farewell piece at Walter's departure for the war, is that in the aftermath of Walter's death Dietrich shifted ambitions so as to come to terms with the death of his brother, his family's grief over his death, and—perhaps—Dietrich's own gnawing guilt for having unwittingly played a piece that would haunt him as a dirge.

The story of Bonhoeffer's lifelong attitude toward music suggests that there was something profound underlying his childhood shift from pianist to pastor. Essentially, after his decision to study theology and before his joyful discovery of polyphony as a metaphor for the love of God in the last year of his life, Bonhoeffer displays an odd ambivalence toward music. On one hand, his writings are full of incidental references to music: he speaks of the role of song in communal Christian life; he chastises American church services for their dreadful music (though he teaches Negro spirituals to his Finkenwalde ordinands); he quotes from hymns in order to make a point—sometimes even scrawling out a staff and penning the melody if the point is less than overt; and, perhaps most important, he continues to play as an evening hobby with like-minded friends. But, on the other hand, virtually all of these references to music in Bonhoeffer's life are "incidental." When added together, of course, they suggest a major interest in the subject, but one always gets the feeling that Bonhoeffer purposely keeps this interest below the surface as though, through disciplined denial, it must be kept at bay in order to leave room for the more important things he devotes his life to.

This, at any rate, is how it appeared to at least one of Bonhoeffer's students. Goebel recalls being startled by seeing his teacher play the piano, for something came over him "which I had not known in him and have never seen again": "an expression of natural force, something primeval." After asking his teacher about it, Goebel concluded that "Bonhoeffer cast this passion out of his life for the sake of the call to a greater 'passion.'"[19] This observation, it is supposed, is part of the complex being spoken of here and anchored in the family milieu of Bonhoeffer's thirteenth and fourteenth year.

The play on the word "passion" runs probably deeper than Goebel suspected. The pun does not seem exhausted by juxtaposing a zestful enthusiasm at the piano with the Passion of Christ. Instead, it seems that "passion" also plays on Bonhoeffer's eventual martyrdom and on the Bonhoeffer family's nurturing within it a kind of Christ figure under an aura of death. However the pun is interpreted, the fact is that the thought of death dominated young Dietrich's reflections when he came to the decision to forgo music and follow Christ. Moreover, his preoccupation with death most certainly had its impetus in the death of his brother, and the family events surrounding it. There are two documents which substantiate this interpretation, one written by Bonhoeffer himself and the other by his twin sister.

Sabine attributes her brother's decision to study theology to a childhood preoccupation with death. In one of several passages on the subject, she writes:

> He and I shared a room between the ages of eight and ten, and at night in bed we had very solemn talks about

death and eternal life. The 1914 war had broken out, and
we heard of the deaths of our grown-up cousins, and the
fathers of our school-fellows. So, after the evening prayers
and singing (which was always shared by our mother
when she was home), we lay awake a long time and tried
to imagine what eternal life and being dead were like.
We endeavored every evening to get a little nearer to
eternity by concentrating on the word "eternity."[20]

Sabine then goes on to note that after the twins were separated
in their own bedrooms her brother would knock on the wall to
remind her of their meditations, though she soon lost interest
and Dietrich, presumably, continued them by himself.

Although this document contributes much to our understanding of Dietrich's earliest motivation to enter the ministry, there is
some question about the dates that Sabine provides. That is, we
are assuming that it was in the aftermath of Walter's death specifically that Dietrich made his childhood decision, and that would
have been 1918; yet Sabine indicates that the meditations began
when the twins were between the ages of eight and ten—that is,
between 1914 and 1916. How can this discrepancy be accounted
for?

Essentially, the conjecture here is that Sabine made the common error of confusing the dates of national history with those
of family history. Specifically, she supposes that since the war
broke out in 1914, it was then that the twins began to think on
death. However, her supposition is not necessarily soundly based
because, as we have seen, the Bonhoeffers were a quite insulated
family and quite possibly the children had little encounter with
the casualties of the war prior to their brothers' service in it, which
occurred toward its end. Indeed, since Sabine did not write this
account for some five and one half decades after the events, it is
very possible that her dates are confused.

But there is more specific evidence that the year that Sabine refers to is 1918 rather than 1914 or 1916. For one thing, two pages later she mentions that Dietrich got his own room at twelve, not at ten. Furthermore, since she indicates that the childhood meditations begun by the twins together were continued by Dietrich alone, and that the duration of these meditations probably did not stretch over years, then it may be safely assumed that the period in question is just before and just after Dietrich was moved to a room of his own. This separation, by Sabine's account, was 1918—the year their brother was killed in the war.

Second, a phrase in Sabine's memoir would be strange if the period in question were not just after Walter's death. This is her comment that the prayers and songs were always shared by her mother "when she was home." Hence the question arises: when was she not at home? Everything we have seen about Paula Bonhoeffer shows that she was the center of the household and probably rarely ventured outside—especially in the evenings, when Sabine implies that she was sometimes not at home. The only solution to this riddle is that the period of the twins' meditation corresponded almost exactly to the period of Paula Bonhoeffer's "weeks" of recuperation in bed at the neighbor's house, for this is the only period we can think of during which she may have been regularly absent at the evening prayers and singing. So, unwittingly, Sabine apparently provides an almost specific date of Dietrich's meditations on death: the weeks and perhaps months immediately following April 1918, when the news of Walter's death had arrived and Paula Bonhoeffer was incapacitated. Indeed, it may also be assumed that it is this specific period that Bonhoeffer later writes of in his allegory of death, for there and here the dead child corresponds chronologically with the absent mother.

Besides Sabine's recollections of their childhood meditations on death, there is another document which discusses this impetus for Bonhoeffer's decision to become a Christian and a theologian.

It is something he wrote around the year 1932, and it most assuredly refers to his own childhood:

> He liked thinking about death. Even in his boyhood he had liked imagining himself on his death-bed, surrounded by all those who loved him, speaking his last words to them. Secretly he had often thought about what he would say at that moment. To him death was neither grievous nor alien. He would have liked to die young, to die a fine, devout death. He would have liked them all to see and understand that to a believer in God dying was not hard, but was a glorious thing.[21]

The author continues, saying that he realized that "he would really have to die one day ... [and] ... from that day on he buried inside himself something about which he did not speak or think again." This realization being the point of the story, we may assume that the "day" occurred in 1932 when Bonhoeffer embarked on the path of discipleship proper and penned the soliloquy. Since that path is the next phase of Bonhoeffer's development in our study, our present interest is in this "death wish" in the adolescent Christian.

Crucial to my thesis is that the death Bonhoeffer speaks of is a "fine," "young," "devout" death and, through it, "he would have liked them all to see and understand that to a believer in God dying was not hard, but was a glorious thing." Here we see the longing of a "chivalrous" boy to sacrifice himself—were it possible—in order to show a family broken by the death of a son that death need not be feared. And, of course, it was the Christian faith's answer to death that enabled him to dream of the solution. This, I argue, is Bonhoeffer's own explanation of why he chose to dedicate his life to the church instead of, say, to music. Completely blind at the time to his own actual mortality, he embraced Christianity for what it promised for a family broken by death—

if the sting could be snatched from death, harmony in his child-hood world could once again prevail. Moreover, since the "ploy" had the willing collaboration of his parents and twin sister, it worked. Paula Bonhoeffer recovered, and mother and son were fused even tighter into a Christian alliance that none dared touch.

If it was out of this family complex that Bonhoeffer became a Christian and decided to devote his life to the church, it is also this complex that propelled him into his specialty in Christian ethics—and indeed contributed to the shape that his ethical reflec-tions would take. As for his attraction to ethics as opposed to, say, church history—which, as late as his inaugural dissertation, adviser Seeberg was suggesting would be an area in which he might make a contribution—we see that Bonhoeffer came to his Christian commitment with a decidedly ethical orientation. It was not simply intellectual curiosity which led him to an interest in theology. Neither was it a concern for the fate of his own soul. Rather, it was the broken human community that led him to see in Chris-tianity a path for reconciliation. Indeed, perhaps the single most striking thing about the above-quoted soliloquy is that its focus is not on death per se—the author's own mortality in particular—but on the way in which an "answer" to death can mend the human community. In this is an implicit ethical orientation with special reference to social ethics. Thus, it is not taken here as accidental that Bonhoeffer erected a moral paradox of costly grace at the beginning of his book on discipleship. For, as has been shown, the cost of grace is most literally death, though death is intimately bound up with the paradox of reasoning about grace and the commitment to sociality generally.

It is a relatively straightforward matter, mentioned by nearly all Bonhoeffer interpreters, to detail the lifelong preoccupation with death that Bonhoeffer evidences in his writings. This preoc-cupation begins to show mostly in 1932, when the path of disci-pleship begins properly. We have quoted from one of his soliloquies of that year, as well as the sermon he preached in which he calls for a new kind of martyr, a guilty martyr, evidencing a premonition of his own death. Indeed, we shall be unable to escape the thesis (to be developed later) that in the political resistance, where Bonhoeffer risked his own death and self-consciously undertook the moral responsibility of assassination, he hit the bedrock of his own psychological constitution and so finally broke free of it. Moreover, it is not incidental that this life-and-death struggle in the resistance was aimed at the goal of preserving a community, Germany, and that it confronted him with an unfathomable moral paradox that he could resolve only in action and not in thought. This existential affinity he feels with death during the resistance is illustrated, among other places, in his privately circulated essay written for the conspirators. There he writes that "fundamentally we feel that we belong to death already," or "we still love life, but I do not think that death can take us by surprise now."[22] What I think the evidence shows is that actually Bonhoeffer "belonged to death" much earlier than that. He was claimed for death in April 1918, and it was this affinity with it that accounts for his lifelong aura of loneliness as well as the character of much of his later thought and action.

But I am also supposing that the motif of death, chiseled into the paradoxical core of discipleship, was intimately bound up with his commitment to sociality, which he expressed both directly and through a critique of instrumental reason. At issue here is not a more or less standard metapsychological "death wish," but the unique sociopsychological nexus of a unique Christian ethic. In *The Cost of Discipleship*, for example, where we read "when Christ calls a man, he bids him to come and die," we read too that "the Christian also has . . . to bear the sins of others; he too must bear their shame and be driven like a scapegoat from the gate of the city." This suffering, which "the Christian is not spared," is the Christian's death he writes about, as it is also "the badge of true discipleship."[23] And this rounds out Bonhoeffer's particular notion of the Christian's death. It is a death that is premised on shame and loneliness (banishment from the city), and a death that reconciles the human community. For, like Christ, the disciple is fundamentally dying for others, suffering an unjust and atoning death. This is the kind of death that Bonhoeffer wished for himself when his family was struck dumb by Walter's death: a sacrificial death that, like Christ's, would prove to his family that death held no sting and so would rectify its fragmented solidarity. And this is also the kind of death that Bonhoeffer eventually did suffer: a martyr's death, stained only by the guilt of solidarity with humanity.

Family, Church, and World

If Bonhoeffer became a theologian and an ethicist in the context of his family, it was nevertheless the church to which he devoted his professional career. And if Bonhoeffer's legacy is the legacy of a churchman, we must also recognize that in his final years it was not primarily the actual church but the world that he was serving. The thesis of this book is designed, of course, to show how the context of his family was a predisposing and enduring one which colored his actions in both the church and the world. But sociopsychological interpretation should never be pressed so far as to devalue, implicitly or explicitly, the actions of an individual in realms that common sense knows to be fundamentally religious or political. To put my point another way, at the same time that we recognize the sociopsychological milieu that molded Bonhoeffer's personality, we must also stand back and appreciate the fact that the thought and action of this man did not remain in the province of the family. It ventured out into realms in which the social psychologist, too, is a religious seeker and political actor. To appreciate these steps Bonhoeffer took outside his family, let us turn to a passage from *Letters and Papers from Prison* which has puzzled Bonhoeffer scholars for years: "I don't think I've ever changed very much, except perhaps at the time of my first impressions abroad and under the first conscious influence of father's personality. It was then that I turned from phraseology to reality."[24] At issue are the one or two—even the number is ambiguous in the text—times that Bonhoeffer understood himself to have changed. Let us consider them briefly for what they reveal about Bonhoeffer's venturings outside the family and into religion and politics.

Bonhoeffer's "first impressions abroad" are the easiest to date and interpret. He first went abroad in 1924 when, together with Klaus, he traveled to Rome and North Africa. The significance of this trip for Bonhoeffer's ecclesiastic commitment is well documented. After attending his first mass in St. Peter's, he recorded in his diary: "I believe I am beginning to understand the concept of the church."[25] Bethge later concludes: "Rome was the first major experience of his student years. It would hardly be an exaggeration to say that the origins of the theological principles of his early period are discernible here."[26] The fact is that Bonhoeffer was enthralled by the splendor of the Roman Catholic Church, considered converting to it, and remained throughout his life a steadfast defender of it, even showing a hesitancy to use the term "church" for what he prefered to call "Protestantism." And, from what we know about the familial roots of his faith, it may be supposed that it was in this awe-inspiring experience of Rome that Bonhoeffer transferred his allegiance from his family to the church. To be sure, this did not sever the bonds of his family over him, but it did provide a context outside the family in which he could enact his struggles and aspirations. Indeed, it is significant that Bonhoeffer writes of this experience as his "first impressions abroad" rather than mentioning Rome per se, for it was perhaps as important that he leave the setting of his family as it was that he discover something new in another church in another land.

It is much harder to make sense of the second change Bonhoeffer mentions, the "first conscious influences of father's personality" which led him to turn "from phraseology to reality." As
recently as November 1984, the *Newsletter* of the English Language
Section of the International Bonhoeffer Society for Archive and
Research carried a brief review of the competing interpretations
of this change.[27] That review pointed out that scholars have dated
this change everywhere from the summer of 1924—making the
change the same as that just discussed—to the early 1940s. I believe
that the debate cannot be resolved by textual analysis alone but
requires that responsible interpretation rely on other, concomitant evidence. More to the point, I think that the variety of dates
is itself an indicator that what we are dealing with is not so much
a fixable date as a progression throughout Bonhoeffer's adult life.

This second change Bonhoeffer records may be equated with
the first only in the sense that his earliest theological impulses
could not be traceable to the influences of his mother without
the influence of his father because, were it not for the relationship
between his parents, his mother's influences would very likely
have been quite different. On the other hand, it is difficult to assert
that in his earliest writings Bonhoeffer already had turned from
phraseology to reality, for the simple fact is that these are quite
unreal, verbose treatises. Unquestionably the search for reality in
them is real, but I do not find it effectively accomplished. By
contrast, most scholars date the change from phraseology to reality
between 1930 and 1932; that is, on the threshold of discipleship.
In the main, this period (and 1932 in particular) strikes me as the
most likely for reasons to be discussed in the next chapter. To
anticipate, I think that the paradox of obedience was worked out
primarily as Bonhoeffer recognized the previously submerged
influence of his father and struggled to deal with it. Moreover,
the very essence of discipleship was to turn from the abstract
theologizing of his earlier works and to anchor his thought in
genuine Christian practice. Furthermore, discipleship was not so

much a recognition of reality as it was a struggle to grasp reality in all its paradoxical dimensions. The attempt was there, but it was not successful. Bonhoeffer's shift from phraseology to reality, then, was not until the 1940s when he joined the political resistance and enacted the paradoxes of discipleship. Here, too, was the only time in his life that he enjoyed a close relationship with his father, brother, and brothers-in-law; it was the first time he was not implicitly at odds with them but joined them in joint action. Thus my suggestion, based upon primarily sociopsychological evidence, is that Bonhoeffer's turn from phraseology to reality under the conscious influence of his father's personality was a progressive one: begun perhaps as early as 1924, raised as a personal dilemma in 1932, resolved only through action in the 1940s—and recognized as a change only in retrospect in 1944.

Of what significance are this debate and my conjectures about it for the present study? The first significant element is political. It is the suggestion that Bonhoeffer not only ventured outside his home into the church, but that he also traveled progressively from the church to the world. Discipleship was the ethic he devised to carry him on this journey, and that is why its near-exclusive focus on the church (and church struggle) finally gave way to a focus on the world. For discipleship was not negated in the political resistance; rather, it was enacted there in its paradoxical dimensions—only after imprisonment did Bonhoeffer acknowledge straightforwardly the limitations of discipleship. Until that time, discipleship was the praxic vehicle which he drove among the three domains of family, church, and world.

The second significance of Bonhoeffer's turn from phraseology to reality is the sociopsychological one he called "the influence of father's personality." Again, I do not suggest that at one time Bonhoeffer awoke and consciously recognized the influence of his father; rather, the awakening was a progressive one. For behind the constellation of forces that led Dietrich to ally with his mother and to take up the challenge posed by Walter's death was the submerged influence of his father. Mediated by the influence of his mother, his father's influence, however indirect, was real. Because it was indirect, his father has been seen only as a counterplayer so far, but because it was real—on a stage set primarily by his mother—it was the influence of his father that troubled Bonhoeffer as he set out upon the path of discipleship. On that path it was the problem of obedience, of "resistance and submission"—as the German and first English title of *Letters and Papers from Prison* aptly characterizes it—with which he wrestled in the events that led through discipleship to political resistance.

IV

The Path of Discipleship

In 1932, at age twenty-six, Bonhoeffer stood on the threshold of what promised to be a brilliant career. In the four years since he had earned his doctorate from perhaps the world's leading theological faculty he had served as an assistant pastor in Spain, completed his inaugural dissertation, and spent a year as a post-doctoral fellow at Union Theological Seminary in New York City. Upon his return from the United States, he had met Karl Barth, had taken up his first pastor's duties following his ordination in the fall of 1931, had entered the ecumenical movement, and had begun lecturing at the University of Berlin. There were, of course, dismal social conditions to be reckoned with and fears of ominous

political developments, but—as yet—these signs of coming catas-
trophe had not encroached directly upon the lives of theologians
and teachers, or upon the institutions they served. In all, Bonhoeffer showed remarkable professional promise and had everything to look forward to.

Yet 1932 was a discomforting year for Bonhoeffer, and the
symptom of his discomfort was depression. Indeed, though there
is hardly an exhaustive account of each instance of it, Bethge
reports that depression was a kind of recurrent malaise for his
mentor. And, while we can be reasonably certain that 1932 was
not the first time Bonhoeffer became so afflicted, there is every
reason to suppose that his depression in this year was worse than
before. In 1932 Bonhoeffer plunged headlong into a search for
"origins": his personal origins, as revealed by his soliloquies of
the year, and theological origins, as revealed by his 1933 University
of Berlin lectures. This search suggests that around 1932 he was
using his depression as an impetus to re-evaluate his commitments
by explicating their sources and foundations. Moreover, as discussed previously, there is reason to believe that this year, too,
was a watershed year for his coming to grips with a father's influence that before had reached him only indirectly through the
mediation of his mother. And, finally, we know that this year marks
the beginning of the path of discipleship proper. Thus, it can be
supposed that in the personal crises of 1932 and thereabouts, the
ethic we know today as discipleship was being forged.

Of the three paradoxes of the ethic of discipleship presented
in chapter I, one and part of another were present in Bonhoeffer's
thought prior to 1932. These were his commitment to the sociality
of Christ and costly grace, in the sense that the cost of grace was
death. His dissertation established his lifelong commitment to
sociality, and the sermon preached in the summer of 1932 which
included the call for guilty martyrdom established the death motif
in his thought. As for the second dimension of the paradox of

costly grace, the critique of instrumental reason, that was the last addition to *The Cost of Discipleship,* added only upon the writing of the publication draft. Indeed, it is only in the drafts of the *Ethics* that we begin to understand his idea of costly grace as a critique of instrumental reason, though even there we must draw parallels that he did not draw for us. Nevertheless, even if ill-articulated, the critique of instrumental reason may be said to be present in Bonhoeffer's earliest commitment to sociality, insofar as the critique is essentially a call for a practical, social reason. Thus, the only aspect of discipleship that in 1932 was yet to be added to the ethic was the paradox of obedience. Theologically this is probably the least important paradox of discipleship, for it asserts little substantively. Most simply, after all, the paradox of obedience is a critique of a mere verbal-conventional profession of faith, a critique suggested by the overt meaning of costly grace, constituting a call to follow and to make oneself truly a disciple of Christ. But, existentially, it is probably the most crucial aspect of discipleship, for it is the paradox of obedience that infuses discipleship with its praxic, active dimension. The paradox of obedience is not so much a theological proposition as it is a call for action. It is the existential spark that ignites the other paradoxes and causes them to move. In short, the paradox of obedience, introduced into Bonhoeffer's thought after 1932, is the element of discipleship that harnesses the other paradoxes and infuses them with existential urgency.

The overall strategy of this chapter is to link the development of the paradox of obedience with Bonhoeffer's progressive recognition of the influence of his father. This influence, as Bonhoeffer himself asserted, is what induced Bonhoeffer to change from phraseology to reality. And that shift marks the importance of the paradox of obedience for discipleship, for it is obedience to Christ in the world that enables discipleship to link faith and worldly action. That is, discipleship is an ethic that seeks to relate faith to the empirical world, and the paradox of obedience and belief is what makes such a relationship possible insofar as it prevents either the dichotomization of faith and works or the subordination of one to the other. Thus, it is the paradox of obedience that accounts for the quest of the disciple to lodge the reality of faith in worldly reality. Recall here my conclusion that the ethic of discipleship is not entirely successful in tapping this twofold reality (Bonhoeffer's partial distancing from *The Cost of Discipleship* in 1944 suggests that he, too, ultimately thought that discipleship was not entirely successful). Nonetheless, what is important about discipleship is that it represents a progressively successful search by Bonhoeffer to lodge faith in the world of action—that is, to appreciate "reality." Again, my thinking is that Bonhoeffer grasps reality only at the culmination of discipleship where, in political resistance, he enacts the role of disciple and so paradoxically both fulfills and negates it. In sum, the importance of discipleship is that it is the ethic that guided Bonhoeffer along the path that finally allowed him to turn from phraseology to reality. Accordingly, the aim of this chapter is to chronicle the psychological dimension of this journey in Bonhoeffer's progressive awareness of the influence of his father's personality over him.

Specifically, four challenges are faced in this chapter, each of which enables us to appreciate Bonhoeffer's progressive awareness and his concomitant progressive realism. First, Bonhoeffer's 1933 lectures on theological origins are discussed for the light they shed on his dawning awareness of the implicit conflict in his theological origins, an awareness traceable, in part, to the implicit conflict between his mother and father. Second, the general case for Bonhoeffer's conflict with his father is made, and it is supposed that this conflict was generalized by him to authority figures in general. Third, the relationship between Bonhoeffer and Karl Barth is examined by looking at letters exchanged between them. Here it is assumed that a certain transference phenomenon was in operation wherein Bonhoeffer projected some of his feelings regarding his father onto Barth and, by so doing, worked through the worst of them. Finally, the motives for Bonhoeffer's entrance into the political conspiracy are discussed. It is shown that Bonhoeffer's political actions were, in large part, motivated by his desire to pay his psychological debt to his family and, in particular, to come to grips with his ambivalence toward his father and his struggle with submission and rebellion generally. Here, in the climax of discipleship, is the last time we see Bonhoeffer ensnared by his family.

Establishing the Problematic:
Lectures on Origins

When Bonhoeffer embarked upon the path of discipleship in 1932, he did not appear to be aware that it was the influence of his father's personality which catapulted him into fashioning a novel ethic. That recognition came only a dozen years later, after he had spent a solitary year of introspection in prison. Prior to this 1944 recognition—and probably dating from his impressions of Rome where he transferred his allegiance from his family to the church—Bonhoeffer couched the bulk of even his personal reflections in the language of the Christian. It is not surprising, therefore, that although he recognized the personal dimensions of his struggles in 1932, he seems to have transferred at least some of the energy emanating from these struggles into the theological arena. Indeed, assuming that discipleship was fashioned in a family context, we would expect to see such a transfer.

It is interesting, therefore, that in the same year that Bonhoeffer found himself perplexed by the question of his own "origins"—

a question he would only later answer by reference to his father's influence—he chose to give a series of lectures at the University of Berlin on the problem of theological "origins" (published as *Creation and Fall*). Given the thesis developed so far, one has reason to suspect that in these 1932 lectures Bonhoeffer would set the stage for the problem that he intended to address with discipleship, and that this problem would be simultaneously a personal and a theological one. And the stage-setting, it appears, is exactly what happened.

Creation and Fall takes as its focus an anthropological inter-pretation of Genesis 1–3, or "origins." As might be expected, Bonhoeffer's point of departure is human sociality: "Man is not alone," he argues, "but it is in the dependence on the other that his creatureliness consists."[1] It follows (again not surprisingly from the author of *The Communion of Saints*) that obedience to God and harmony in creation requires the just arrangement of this human community. Conversely, however, Bonhoeffer identifies sin as the violation of the human other whose "limit" is trans-gressed by hedonism. Such a transgression—in terms Buber pop-ularized, though they describe Bonhoeffer's meaning as well—creates an "I–it" relationship where there should be an "I–Thou" relationship. The result is sin.

But Bonhoeffer's task in *Creation and Fall* is more than a reiteration of earlier theses; instead, he wants to delve into the *origins* of human transgression—that is, "original sin." Interest-ingly for a familial interpretation, these origins reside for Bon-hoeffer in the division of the sexes. That is, for the Bonhoeffer of *Creation and Fall*, primal human sociality is found in the division of the sexes and, as a consequence, so is primal sin. Translating *tob* and *ra* of the tree of knowledge as closer to "pleasure" and "pain" than "good" and "evil," he puts the matter this way:

> The knowledge of *tob* and *ra* is originally not an ab-
> stract knowledge of ethical principles, but sexuality; i.e.,

a perversion of the relationship between persons. And since the essential nature of sexuality consists in destruction[,] the dark secret of the originally sinful being of man is in fact preserved from generation to generation in continuing procreation.[2]

The premise of this argument is, of course, that sexual relations may not transpire without overstepping the rightful limits of another, no matter how well intentioned the initiation of the act was.

Now, be the actual argument of *Creation and Fall* as it may, it is striking that in this year of personal and theological search for "origins," Bonhoeffer located the origins of sin in the relationship between man and woman. Previously—that is, in *The Communion of Saints*—he had told us that the church was most like the family, but not until 1932 does he actually locate the potentiality (and inevitability) of sin in the family unit. The inference here, then, must be that, whatever he was saying theologically, Bonhoeffer in 1932 was personally and painfully aware of a conflict existing in the union of man and woman.

All of this hypothesis is plausible when it is remembered that years later Bonhoeffer would attribute this turning point in his life to a recognition of his father's influence over him. The reason this makes sense is that, in forming an alliance with his mother during his childhood and youth, there was an at least implicit conflict with his father, who, it will be remembered, did not share his wife's or son's enthusiasm for Christianity. Now, if in 1932 Bonhoeffer was beginning to recognize the influence of his father, it follows that he would also recognize the implicit conflict between his mother and father. It may not have been an overt conflict—and, indeed, all the evidence suggests that Christianity was rarely debated in the Bonhoeffer family unless a spirit of tolerance prevailed—but it was nonetheless a conflict. Moreover, since Bonhoeffer was a male child and as such was destined to enter the male world of his father—even if he did so as a theologian—it must be supposed that he came to embody this conflict between his mother and father. In other words, what Bonhoeffer shows us in *Creation and Fall* is that in 1932 he not only recognized the influence of his father, but also recognized that this influence—combined with that of his mother—was the source of conflict for him. What must be examined, therefore, for an understanding of the immediate catalyst for discipleship, is not merely the influence of Bonhoeffer's father over him set against a backdrop of his mother's influence, but also the conflict that this influence engendered in the twenty-six-year-old theologian. This conflict, born in a distant and cordial relationship between father and son, was, it appears, generalized to authority in general.

Conflict with Authority

It already has been shown how the relationship between Karl and Dietrich Bonhoeffer contained an implicit if not explicit conflictual edge. Also shown has been the fact that both Karl-Friedrich and Klaus tended to follow their father's footsteps on matters of faith, and so left little brother Dietrich with no male support in the household for his religious views. And, to make matters worse, whereas Karl Bonhoeffer was at least polite enough to hold his opinions to himself, the elder Bonhoeffer brothers were not. They railed against their little brother's choice of vocation, and so voiced what Dietrich probably only felt from his father. And—as though a foretaste of what would follow—Dietrich's childhood response to his brothers' accusations of the feebleness of the church is reported to have been: "Then I shall reform the church!" In this remembrance from childhood in the Bonhoeffer home is crystallized the result that Bonhoeffer's conflict with authority would later have.

But what has not yet been shown is the extent to which this conflict pervaded Dietrich's life, or its effect on his own inner motivations as a child embarking upon the study of theology.

The conflict that appears to have begun with Bonhoeffer's relationship with his father and brothers also appears to have accompanied him into other areas of his life. We already have seen, for example, the difficulties Bonhoeffer evidenced in peer relationships. As a boy and a young man, he rarely made a friend, and his father reported his childhood tendency to have been to fight a bit too much. Then, too, his fellow student in New York found Bonhoeffer to have an unattractive aristocratic temperament that kept likely friends at bay. We have observed also the fact that Bonhoeffer's friends, when made, were typically drawn from his juniors and intellectual inferiors. And, finally, lest we make too much out of his experiment with communal living at Finkenwalde, it must be acknowledged that, whatever the pretense, Bonhoeffer was the recognized and appointed leader of the seminary; often it is those who have most difficulty with personal relationships yet yearn for them that are attracted to experiments in communal living. In short, evidence from Bonhoeffer's relationships with peers suggests a profound uneasiness with mutuality, which is a likely indicator of a more general conflict with authority.

But evidence for an enduring conflict with authority comes not only from Bonhoeffer's lifelong inability to effect mutuality in personal relationships; it comes also from what appears to have been an almost pitiful fear of authority figures. We need only to remember his non-choice of a professor —Seeberg, who would exert less influence over him, rather than the likes of a Harnack or a Barth, who claimed more of his respect. Indeed, the story of his relationship, or lack of relationship, with Barth will be detailed below when we discuss Bonhoeffer's attempts to overcome this conflict with authority, but parts of this story could fit here as well. And then, during his period of lecturing at the University of Berlin, when faced with the disapproval of his elder colleagues, he claimed to prefer the company of his students and proceeded to write the whole affair off in favor of practical work. But even in his practical work, Bonhoeffer appears never to have really subordinated himself to an authority. He always seemed at a distance from direct supervision and, in general, went his own way even in the face of objections, such as at Finkenwalde. In all, Bonhoeffer seems to have been as incapable of working with an older man as he was with peers, and it can be supposed that the root of both circumstances resided in the conflict with authority that carried over from his relationship with his father and brothers.

Having seen, then, that the conflict Bonhoeffer experienced with his father and brothers probably foreshadowed his other relationships, the question arises: how did it influence his thought? To begin with, it will be remembered that there was quite a bit of authoritarianism in Bonhoeffer's thought, probably traceable to his personal conflict with authority. Since the following section of this chapter is devoted to discussing how his orientation worked itself out in the ethic of discipleship, here a prior question is addressed: how did a conflict with authority influence Bonhoeffer's earliest theological impulses? With this question we return, in part, to the issues addressed in the last chapter. However, whereas the intention there was to trace the primary early influences on Bonhoeffer's theological beginnings, the intention here is to flesh out what was a partially one-sided view. The task is made much simpler by a soliloquy of Bonhoeffer's, written in 1932, which reflects, albeit indirectly, on the influence his father had on his original theological vision. Let us consider this document at length:

> One day in the first form, when the master asked him what he wanted to study, he quietly answered theology, and flushed. The word slipped out so quickly that he did not even stand up. Having the teacher's gaze and that of

the whole class directed at him personally and not at his work, and being suddenly called upon to speak out like this, gave him such conflicting feelings of vanity and humility that the shock led to an infringement of ordinary class behavior, an appropriate expression of the consternation caused by the question and the answer. The master obviously thought so too, for he rested his gaze on him for only a moment longer than usual and then quickly and amiably released him.

He was nearly as disconcerted as his pupil. "In that case you have more surprises to come," he said, speaking just as quietly. Actually the question "how long?" had been on his lips, but, as if that would have touched on the secret of his own early and passionately begun and then quickly dropped study of theology—and also because he felt displeased with himself at having nothing better to say to a boy whom he had known and liked for a long time—he grew embarassed, cleared his throat, and went back to the Greek text which was the subject of the lesson.

The boy absorbed that brief moment deep into himself. Something extraordinary had happened, and he enjoyed it and felt ashamed at the same time. Now they all knew, he had told them. Now he was faced with the riddle of his life. Solemly he stood there in the presence of his God, in the presence of his class. He was the centre of attention. Did he look as he wanted to look, serious and determined? He was filled with an unusual sense of well-being at the thought, though he immediately drove it away, realizing the grandeur of his confession and his task. Nor did it escape him at that moment that he had caused the master a certain embarrassment, though at the same time he had looked at him with pleasure and approval. The moment swelled into pleasure, the class-room expanded into the infinite. There he stood in the midst of the world as the herald and teacher of his knowledge and ideals, they all had now to listen to him in silence, and the blessing of the Eternal rested on his words and on his head. And again he felt ashamed. For he knew about his pitiful vanity.

How often he had tried to master it. But it always crept back again, and it spoilt the pleasure of this moment. Oh, how well he knew himself at the age of seventeen. He knew all about himself and his weaknesses. And he also knew that he knew himself well. And through the corner of that piece of self-knowledge his deep vanity again forced an entry into the house of his soul and made him afraid.

It had made a tremendous impression on him when he had read in Schiller that man needed only to rid himself of a few small weaknesses to be like the gods. Since then he had been on the watch. He would emerge from the struggle like a hero, he said to himself. He had just made a solemn vow to do so. The path that he had known that he must follow since the age of fourteen was clearly marked out for him. But supposing he failed? Supposing the struggle proved vain? Supposing he was not strong enough to see it through?

The words "You have more surprises to come" suddenly rang in his ears. Surprises about what? What did he mean? What was the meaning of the curious, mistrustful, bored, disappointed, mocking eyes of his class-mates? Didn't they credit him? Didn't they believe in his honesty? Did they know something about him that he did not know himself?

Why are you all looking at me like that? Why are you embarrassed, sir? Look away from me, for heaven's sake, denounce me as a mendacious, conceited person who does not believe what he says. Don't keep so considerately silent, as if you understood me. Laugh aloud at me, don't be so abominably dumb—it's intolerable.

There is the throng. He stands in the midst of it and speaks, fervently, passionately. He corrects himself. A leaden silence lies over the throng, a dreadful, silent mockery. No, it cannot be. He is not the man they take him to be. He really is in earnest. They have no right to scorn me. They are doing him wrong, all of them. He prays.

God, say yourself whether I am in earnest about you. Destroy me now if I am lying. Or punish them all; they are my enemies, and yours. They do not believe me. I know myself I am not good. But I know it myself—and you, God, know it too. I do not need the others. I, I. I shall win. Do you see their consternation? I am with you. I am strong. God, I am with you.

Do you hear me? Or do you not? To whom am I speaking? To myself? To you? To those others here?

Who is that speaking? My faith or vanity?

God, I shall study theology. Yes, I have said so, and they all heard it. There is no more retreat. I shall . . . but if . . . ?

And as [illegible] tries to think about something else, all he hears is the form master's voice from a distance, saying, "Aren't you feeling well? You don't look well." He pulls himself together, stands up, and as usual begins construing the difficult Greek text."[3]

This confrontation of Bonhoeffer's with the "riddle of his life" fleshes out the character of his theological beginnings discussed in the last chapter. There it was shown how the dominant influence on Bonhoeffer's decision to become a theologian and an ethicist derived from his mother, and especially from his relationship with his mother in the aftermath of Walter's death. Here, however, we see what must have been the implication of that scenario for Bonhoeffer's relationship with his father—and how *this* crept in to influence, if latently so, his thought. That is, we see the raw force Bonhoeffer released in announcing his vocational decision in the male milieu of his household, as we see how his determination threatened to become vanity. For the key comment in this passage is probably: "Nor did it escape him at that moment that he had caused the master a certain embarrassment, though at the same time he had looked at him with pleasure and approval." Here was the conflictual edge of Bonhoeffer's youthful decision to study theology: he would excel at it, and for this excellence his father and brothers could be proud; but that his vocation was theology would add embarrassment to their pleasure, for it implied a critique of their own careers. Indeed, as though to set the stage for the conflict, the usually well-behaved boy forgets (refuses?) to stand up when addressing the master, a sign of his subtle rebelliousness. And, although the encounter is ostensibly set in the schoolroom, Bethge argues that it could not actually have taken place there, but that the setting is a fictionalized one for what, in fact, occurred in the Bonhoeffer family. Thus, though youthful rebelliousness was not the primary impetus for Bonhoeffer's career decision, this soliloquy juxtaposed with the material presented in the last chapter attests to the festering conflict in his early decision— a conflict which, in 1932 when this passage was written, would come back to haunt the pastor on the brink of discipleship.

All of this evidence shows that there was in Bonhoeffer the psychological temptation to what previous writers have called authoritarianism. This temptation is revealed in passages like the one just quoted—as well as the biographical accounts—revealing a simultaneous fear and awe of authority which, on one hand, contributes to an impulse to submission and, on the other hand, is likely to erupt in acts of tyranny in the subject himself. Both of these potentialities have already been observed in Bonhoeffer's case. Moreover, the reason for this temptation also appears clear: Bonhoeffer's psychological distance from his father and, along with him, his elder brothers and similar male authority figures. This, again, is not to say that Karl Bonhoeffer was himself a tyrannical patriarch. But what is clear is that, owing to the particularities of Bonhoeffer's development—his closeness to his mother and concomitant distance from his father intensified by the reactions to Walter's death—Karl Bonhoeffer was *perceived* by his last son as, in certain respects, tyrannical. And, again, this perception owes as much to Bonhoeffer's own distance from his father as it does to Karl Bonhoeffer's actual behavior or attitude. For at issue is a constellation of family events that threatened family solidarity and so ipso facto discredited family authority, which is dependent upon solidarity for its legitimacy. In this way, the otherwise just authoritarianism of the patriarch came perilously close to unjust authoritarianism or tyranny, and the internalization of this paternal crisis in Dietrich's psyche caused him to evidence a lifelong ambivalence toward authority. And yet our task is not only to observe this ambivalence but to show how, in the period of discipleship, Bonhoeffer strove to address and conquer it. For this we turn to his relationship with Karl Barth.

The Relationship with Barth

In broad strokes, this book's argument is already completed. Having observed a conflict with authority born in the subject's relationship with his father, a sociopsychological interpretation can do no more now than watch the story unfold with an eye to Bonhoeffer's working through his ambivalence toward authority. And this story, for the most part, already has been told. We already have seen that in response to authority, Bonhoeffer chose the path of submission. As illustrated by his 1935 letter to his brother Karl-Friedrich, quoted at the outset of this book, Bonhoeffer believed it would be the power of submission, as expressed in the Sermon on the Mount, that would be capable of crushing Nazi tyranny. We have seen, also, how Bonhoeffer set out practicing this submission. Professionally, until his call came to direct the seminary at Finkenwalde, he withdrew from the church struggle to take pastorates in England. Then, when his opportunity to return arose, he instituted an almost monastic style of communal living at Finkenwalde, thinking that in such an endeavor the power of the faith would be unleashed. Indeed, he practiced meditation and personal confession, and he espoused the values of pacifism. Moreover, he came very close to journeying to India to study with Gandhi, and he did visit monastic Christian communities in England when he had the chance. In all, the change that discipleship effected in Bonhoeffer was one of seeking to squelch his domineering impulses through radical Christian obedience and submission to his fellow man. This quest, undoubtedly, had roots in his discontentment over his own ambivalence toward authority, rooted in his relationship with his father.

Actually the phenomenon being described is not a novel one in the study of the psychology of religious ethicists. "A characteristic of young great rebels," writes Erikson in his monograph on Luther, is

> their inner split between the temptation to surrender and the need to dominate. A great young rebel is torn between on the one hand tendencies to give in and phantasies of defeat (Luther used to resign himself to an early death at times of impending success), and the absolute need, on the other hand, to take the lead, not only over himself but over all the forces and people who impinge on him. In men of ideas the second, dictatorial trend, may manifest

itself paradoxically at first in seeming surrender to passivity which, in the long run, proves to have been an active attempt at liquidating passivity by becoming fully acquainted with it. Even at the time of his near downfall, he struggles for a position in which he can regain a sense of initiative by finding some rock bottom to stand on, after which he can proceed with a total re-evaluation of the premises on which his society is founded.[4]

Now, the parallel between Bonhoeffer and Luther is not a strict one, though the differences between their two cases must await the conclusion of this study. What is important to observe here is how discipleship was, in many ways, impelled by this kind of submissive reaction to authoritarian impulses. Its other elements, which were quite unlike Lutheranism, etched its uniqueness on the history of Christian ethics, yet in the element of submission—born in a conflict with authority rooted in the relationship with the father—the two were quite alike.

But even if it can be shown that Bonhoeffer's chosen path had a certain precedent in religious ethics, the fact remains that there is no way to demonstrate that the psychological disposition born in his family "caused" Bonhoeffer's development of discipleship. Again, the best that can be done is to show how certain factors predisposed its development and the shape it would take; that it took such shape, of course, was Bonhoeffer's doing.

Still, there is one approach that, if not showing the sociopsychological "causes" of discipleship, does help to show its sociopsychological "coordinates." What I have in mind is the description of a sociopsychological trajectory which ran *parallel* to discipleship, without being it or causing it, but which suggests through analogy what it was like. Such a description will then "overlay" discipleship, helping to make its personal, social psychological contours more visible.

An ideal candidate for such a descriptive account of Bonhoeffer's personal path of discipleship is his relationship with Karl Barth during this period, as revealed by their published correspondence. This relationship was undoubtedly the one in which Bonhoeffer most thoroughly re-enacted his childhood conflict with authority and thereby, in part, worked through it. Indeed, my assumption is that the working out of conflicts in this relationship paralleled their working out in discipleship. And such an assumption depends, in large part, on a further assumption of a kind of "transference" by Bonhoeffer between his relationship with his father and his relationship with Barth. This assumption appears plausible on the basis of Bonhoeffer's initial reactions to meeting with Barth. Next, I want to show how Bonhoeffer worked through his simultaneous impulses to both submission and rebellion with Barth. And, finally, I want to look at the measure of freedom that Bonhoeffer achieved as a result of this process that enabled him to return to the source of the original conflict—his father and brothers—with a new-found liberation allowing him to join with them for the first time as a peer and an equal. That this new-found ability for "brotherhood" had as its setting the most rigorous of all brotherhoods—the brotherhood of conspiracy—makes this dimension of the story an especially challenging one.

Bonhoeffer's first encounter with Karl Barth came through the latter's writings in about 1925, and Barth's theological influence on both *The Communion of Saints* and *Act and Being* is strong if qualified. Not until 1931, however, did Bonhoeffer actually meet Barth. The occasion was his return from the United States when he stopped off to see Barth before returning to Berlin. Immediately Bonhoeffer felt a deep attraction to Barth, and he barely made it back to Berlin in time for lectures because of wishing to stay under Barth's teaching. Indeed, Bethge claims that it was "only the occasion of his encounter with Karl Barth" in which Bonhoeffer evidenced an "enthusiasm" for an "outstanding personality."[5] Moreover, in a letter Bonhoeffer wrote to a fellow student, Erwin Sutz, upon his first meeting with Barth, he laments never having met up with an older man "who would really be my teacher." This is what Bonhoeffer wrote: "There's really someone [Barth] that one can get things out of! And to think that I'm sitting in poor old Berlin and moping because there's no one to learn theology from—and so many other useful things in the bargain."[6] And, in the same letter he exclaims: "I don't think that I have ever regretted anything that I have failed to do in my theological past as much as the fact that I did not come here earlier." But, at the same time, Bonhoeffer answers his own lament: it is not only theology that is attracting him to Barth, but also the "so many other useful things." And it is undoubtedly these things, together with Barth's impressive theological exposition, that force Bonhoeffer to mention in a letter from the same period that Barth "looked terrifying."[7] This terror alongside the powerful attraction suggests that the encounter between the two men touched something deep in the psychology of at least the younger. For what Bonhoeffer evidenced upon encountering Barth was nothing less than an almost instantaneous reaction of the sort that we have supposed he had with his father. Probably Bonhoeffer, readied by the completion of his studies and entrance into his vocation, found in Barth the first admirable example of his mother's religious sensibilities and his father's hard-nosed realism. This recognition was, of course, in large part a self-recognition—for Bonhoeffer saw in Barth many of his own submerged aspirations—but because the recognition was effected through an actual relationship, we are probably justified in speaking of it as a kind of transference.

Tracing the course of this relationship through their correspondence offers not a little insight into the personal struggles with authority that the disciple was waging. After these first meetings, for example, Bonhoeffer reveals in a Christmas letter to Barth his initial reaction to their relationship. The tone of ingratiation, and even of adoration, in this letter cannot be missed, and it reveals that Bonhoeffer's first reaction was one of almost authoritarian submission. He writes that "the evening here in Berlin and then the unforgettably splendid hours with you on the Bergli are among the moments in this year which will always be with me." Then, asking to be "excused" if he was a "burden" to Barth, he explains: "I know no one else who can free me from these persistent questions as you can, and that I have to talk to you like that because I feel with you, it is hard to say why, in a strange way quite certain that the way in which you see things is somehow right. I never get the feeling in anything like the same intensity anywhere else."[8] Here Bonhoeffer is quite plain that for him the relationship is not purely intellectual or professional, but is also one of intense and unexplainable feeling. Indeed, it is the feeling which leads him to be "certain" that Barth's views are "somehow right." And, reiterating his appreciation, he closes the letter by thanking Barth once again for his "guiding" of his thoughts in "the brief hours we have been together."

To this letter Barth replies with appreciation for Bonhoeffer's "exposing" of himself on his behalf in Berlin as well as with news of his itinerary. Bonhoeffer then writes again, inquiring about rumors that Barth will be dismissed at Bonn for his anti-Nazi stance and offering to start up a petition on his behalf to prevent this. He adds that "we think of you a great deal" and thanks him again for "the evening in Berlin." To this Barth sends a perfunctory reply stating that all is well with his situation and so a petition is not necessary.

Bonhoeffer's intensity of emotion in this initial stage of his relationship with Barth, or the fact that it was met with curt if courteous responses, could not have gone unnoticed by him.

Instead, as will be shown below, Bonhoeffer was only too aware of the irrational attraction he felt toward Barth, and he began in 1933 to do something about it: he withdrew. Aware that he was very nearly incapable of taking independent action vis-à-vis Barth, and disgusted with himself, he withdrew from the German church struggle to take up pastorates in England. However, just before he withdrew to England, an event transpired that probably etched Bonhoeffer's disgust with himself over his willing entrapment by Barth deep into his conscience. He characteristically had been arguing that the "Aryan Clauses" could not be tolerated by the church, and that the church must take immediate, direct, and unequivocal action against them. But, for the most part, Bonhoeffer was arguing his case alone, so he set out to enlist the aid of Barth. There was an exchange of letters between the two in September of 1933 on the question of the church's proper response to the "Aryan Clauses," and it was during this exchange that Barth urged Bonhoeffer to wait for "a still more central point" on which to base Christian opposition to the Reich. Although surely a frustration for Bonhoeffer, who felt that the entire Christian message stood or fell on the basis of the Church's right to ordain whom it willed—the point denied by the "Aryan Clauses"—he nevertheless could not muster the fortitude to oppose Barth on this crucial matter. This failure undoubtedly unnerved Bonhoeffer, who witnessed in himself his own terror of Barth and impulse to submission, and so, out of disgust with himself as well as the German church, he left for England to begin work in earnest on his theology of discipleship.

It is significant that so well did Bonhoeffer know his own temptation to submission to Barth at this time that he purposely neglected to inform Barth of his move to England. He knew, that is, that Barth would disapprove, and he knew that in the face of this disapproval he could not muster the courage to go. So he chose the easy way out, and left without informing Barth. Not till six weeks later, on 24 October 1933, did Bonhoeffer tell Barth of his new position. In his letter, he implied anticipation of disapproval as his reason for silence:

> I am now writing a letter to you which I wanted to write six weeks ago and perhaps at that time would have resulted in a completely different turn to my personal life. Why I did not write to you then is now almost incomprehensible to me. I only know that there were two contributory factors. I knew that you were busy . . . and . . . the outward condition of one person seemed to me so utterly insignificant. . . . Secondly, I believe that there was also a bit of anxiety about it; I knew that I would have to do what you told me and I wanted to remain free; I simply withdrew myself. I know now that that was wrong, and I must ask you to forgive me. . . . I wanted to ask you whether I should go to London as a pastor or not. I simply believed that you would tell me the right thing, you, and only you.[9]

The letter went on to give Bonhoeffer's reasons for taking up the London pastorates. His stated reasons were simply heeding a call to the ministry and unwillingness to serve a church that excluded non-Aryans. Interestingly, Bonhoeffer had second-guessed his near-mentor well. Ignoring altogether these reasonably valid reasons for moving to England—and, for the first time, playing into Bonhoeffer's private scenario by marshalling some paternal imagery—Barth responds:

> Be glad that I do not have you here in person, for I would let go at you urgently in a quite different way, with the demand that you must now leave go of all these intellectual flourishes and special considerations, however interesting they may be, and think only of one thing, that

you are a German, that the house of your church is on
fire, that you know enough and can say what you know
well enough to be able to help and that you must return
to your post by the next ship. As things are, shall we say
the ship after next?[10]

With this exchange of letters, Bonhoeffer severs the relationship
and does not attempt communication with Barth for three solid
years. One can surmise that, even at this distance, Bonhoeffer
remained fearful of the influence Barth held over him, so he made
his withdrawal a complete one. This period of withdrawal, moreover, corresponds to Bonhoeffer's two years in England and his
first year at Finkenwalde—in short, to the time during which he
developed his theology of discipleship. The analogy here is a sharp
one: the path of Christian obedience which led to the ethic of
discipleship was a path on which Bonhoeffer shook free of his
conflict with authority by means of withdrawal and submission.

And this process is, in effect, what Bonhoeffer's long-delayed
letter to Barth, dated 19 September 1936, reveals. In this letter
Bonhoeffer attempts to share with Barth, again, the reasons for
his silence as well as to fill him in on his now-mature theology
of discipleship and its corresponding program at Finkenwalde.
However, he begins the letter with an outright lie. Recalling Barth's
words, "the ship after next," Bonhoeffer writes that "the arrow
did strike home!" He continues, "I think it really was the ship after
next on which I came home." It was, of course, no such thing.
His lying, his very ability to lie to Barth, reveals the measure of
distance he had achieved from this powerful near-mentor.

Bonhoeffer goes on in the letter to give Barth two reasons for
his three years of silence. One is that he felt "somewhat excluded
from your circle by not taking part in your Festschrift," though
he adds the disclaimer that he merely took this as an "objective
verdict" of their respective theological differences.[11] To this Barth

later responds that there was no question of any "objective verdict" but that Bonhoeffer had, in fact, been simply "forgotten."[12] But here Barth does not quite understand his junior. He picks up on and responds to the childlike hurt expressed by Bonhoeffer, but he does not realize that, at this stage of his junior's distancing from him, it is important to Bonhoeffer to perceive an "objective" difference between them, even if it sorrows him. That Bonhoeffer could measure any "objective" difference between himself and Barth attests to the success that discipleship was having on his personal temptation to tyrannical submission.

The letter, however, listed another reason for Bonhoeffer's three years of silence: that there had been a "constant, silent, controversy" brewing between himself and Barth on theological matters, and he had found himself "departing from your views" on the "exposition of the Sermon on the Mount and the doctrine of justification and sanctification."[13] Here, of course, Bonhoeffer is referring to his theology of discipleship, which would culminate less than a year hence in the publication of *The Cost of Discipleship*. That Bonhoeffer found it necessary to make his constant controversy with Barth during this period a "silent" one suggests, again, how the ethic of discipleship was nestled within a personal complex of conflict with authority.

But again, Barth does not quite understand, and he responds:

> You could have written to me with a quiet conscience long ago, even if in the meanwhile you were describing some theological curves which did not run quite parallel to my own. What claim do I have on you, that you should owe me a solemn reckoning? Do you know . . . the only thing I knew about you for a long time after that business of the "ship after next"? The strange news that you intended to go to India to take over from Gandhi or some other friend of God there a spiritual technique.[14]

Although this response lacked a full understanding of the man to whom it was addressed and his conflicts, almost in its naiveté it manages to strike at the crux of the conflict. Says Barth: "What claim do I have on you, that you should owe me a solemn reckoning?" That claim, only dimly perceived by Barth, was the claim that a father has over his son. Bonhoeffer, indeed, owed Barth nothing; but he owed his father a great deal—including a solemn reckoning. Embittered, Barth cannot help but drop a mildly sarcastic comment about Gandhi or "some other friend of God"— perhaps much the same kind of comment that might have been made by Karl Bonhoeffer about his wife's quiet faith (or, indeed, the kind of comment he might have made to his own mother, Julie Bonhoeffer, who, after all, was the one who instilled in her grandson the urge to visit Gandhi). And, as though to continue his mysteriously accurate groping for an interpretation, Barth's letter goes on to charge Bonhoeffer's program at Finkenwalde with a conflict that may well have had roots in Bonhoeffer's family. He writes:

> I must look very carefully to see how the hare runs so that perhaps I shall be able to say to you that I too feel what you are thinking of to be possible.... I read [the advice on meditation adopted at Finkenwalde] carefully, but I can hardly say that I am very happy about it. I cannot go with the distinction in principle between theological work and devotional edification which is evident in this piece of writing and which I can also perceive from your letter. Furthermore, an almost indefinable odour of monastic eros and pathos in the former writing disturbs me.... I still have neither a positive feeling nor a use for it.[15]

In this uneasiness with the distinction between theological work and devotional edification, and then with the pairing of eros and pathos, did Barth perceive a conflict that was born in a conflict between Karl and Paula Bonhoeffer? To assert this perception would be to assert too much, but it is not without interest that at the same time that Barth "hits" upon his paternal role in relation to Bonhoeffer, he also rebukes the younger for a distinction between theology and devotion. An intriguing linkage, for what has been argued up to this point is that it was from his mother that Bonhoeffer learned "devotion," though it was in ambivalent reaction to his father that he found in "theology" a tool of dominance in a male world. That Barth—on whom Bonhoeffer projected portions of this conflict—detected it is revealing.

Be this as it may, the overall point to be noted is the progress that Bonhoeffer can be seen to have made with his struggle with authority, epitomized by his relationship with Barth, between 1931 and 1936. At the beginning of this period the tone of ingratiation is thick. By 1936 it begins to disappear, showing a much more autonomous and self-confident Bonhoeffer. Recently discovered letters from the period 1941 to 1942 fail to show any of the youthful ingratiation of the earliest ones.[16] Indeed, it is not too far down the road from these that Bonhoeffer criticizes Barth's theology as a positivism of revelation.[17] So, in the end, the task that Bonhoeffer set for himself in 1932 was personally successful in resolving his conflict with authority.

But the important thing about this relationship is what it suggests about the ethic that Bonhoeffer was developing alongside it. In 1932, just after meeting Barth and being dangerously captivated by his influence, Bonhoeffer set out to develop the ethic of discipleship. Then, while work was undertaken in earnest on this ethic—personally in England and as a corporate experiment at Finkenwalde—he withdrew from the presence of Barth. Finally, when the ethic had reached a mature formulation, he once again corresponded with Barth and shared with him the fruits of his

labors. This fact of renewed correspondence as well as its substance suggests that discipleship had, in fact, enabled Bonhoeffer
to conquer the worst of his fears about authority. And, this enabling
power of discipleship was undoubtedly its mandate for radical
Christian obedience; this is the sort of thing that could be learned
in the working through of conflicts with authority rooted in the
experience of a benevolent patriarch who, nevertheless, remained
at arm's length.

Familial Obedience and Political Resistance

The problem of obedience which Bonhoeffer struggled with in
the ethic of discipleship came to a desperate crescendo in 1939.
At issue, again, were competing claims on his loyalty. On one
hand, there was the government—unjust to be sure, but an "order
of creation" to which the Christian owed obedience—and in 1939
it looked as though the National Socialist government was about
to draft Bonhoeffer into the military. But Bonhoeffer's Christian
convictions, already bordering on pacifism, dictated to him that
he could not in good conscience serve in the armed forces of his
country at that time. On the other hand, though, there was the
matter of obedience to his church—the remnant of the Confessing
Church in 1939. As part of their propaganda against the Confessing
Church, the Nazis had accused it of lacking in patriotism. If Bonhoeffer, a recognized leader in the Confessing Church, refused
military service, his refusal would be construed as substantiating
the Nazi accusation that the Confessing Church was anti-German,
and this might strike the death blow to an already crippled church.
Then, too, in Bonhoeffer's personal life there was the matter of
loyalty to his family. He had, until then, carved out an independent

niche for himself in the church struggle and so shared his family's opposition to National Socialism without directly participating in the political resistance they had already committed themselves to. But by 1939 this aloof posture with regard to political action was increasingly impossible to sustain. Most poignantly, the Confessing Church was all but demolished and the political terror mounted: the "crystal night" had been in November 1938, and just two months earlier Bonhoeffer's own twin sister had had to flee the country in the dark of night. In short, the events of 1939 pressured Bonhoeffer into difficult decisions.

Early in 1939 Bonhoeffer hit upon a solution to his dilemmas, and an eminently rational solution at that. Through Reinhold Niebuhr, with whom he had studied during his postdoctoral fellowship at Union Theological Seminary in New York during 1930–31, he requested and received an appointment in the United States, which, happily, was approved by the German government, too. The position entailed a year-long lecture tour through American churches, informing them of the situation of the churches in Germany and of pastoral responsibilities to German refugees. It was, to be sure, the work of a political exile, but, especially when compared with the prospects for most immigrants, it was meaningful professional work for a thirty-three-year-old pastor and theologian. It would enable Bonhoeffer to escape the dilemmas his home country held for him and at the same time to contribute to the causes he held dear by being granted an international pulpit. Moreover, since he already had spent a year in the United States and had at least a few friends and acquaintances there, his transition would be comparatively smooth.

It is because of the rational appeal of the American invitation that we must establish the year 1939 as the time Bonhoeffer self-consciously chose to enter the political resistance. This is so because, rather than remain in America, Bonhoeffer no sooner arrived than he returned to Germany—against the pleadings of his hosts and in disregard of their hospitality. There is evidence from several quarters that the return to Germany in 1939 indicated his decision to enter the political resistance. First, recalling his reported motive for the American exile in the first place—namely, his dilemma at the prospect of military service—we are forced to ask why this issue suddenly disappeared when he decided to return to Germany. Remembering, too, how he did eventually avoid military service—becoming formally affiliated with the *Abwehr*, an agency for military intelligence though really engaged in counterintelligence resistance activities, through the influence of his brother-in-law, Hans von Dohnanyi—we see the answer beginning to come clear. Obviously, prior to his departure in 1939 Bonhoeffer had discussed the prospects for such an appointment with Dohnanyi and understood it to be one of his options. But early in 1939 he had rejected this alternative, probably because he knew full well that it implicated him squarely in the conspiracy. By 1939 his family was actively plotting resistance, and early in 1938 Bonhoeffer himself made his first contacts with the political conspiracy. What must be inferred, therefore, is that an option Bonhoeffer rejected early in 1939—political conspiracy—was the option he tacitly embraced when he decided to return to Germany later that year. To be sure, it was not until 1940 that Bonhoeffer's affiliation with the *Abwehr* became official, and not until 1941 that he made his first journey for counterintelligence purposes, but it seems clear that his moral decision was made in 1939.

Evidence exists in another quarter, too. Hellmut Traub, who met Bonhoeffer prior to his departure for America and immediately after his return, writes that he observed a definite change in Bonhoeffer's political attitude. At their second meeting, Traub reports that Bonhoeffer explained his return to Germany by outlining two courses of action a German of that time might take. One was to fight for Germany at the cost of freedom and Christianity; the other was to work for freedom and Christianity and the defeat of Germany. Says Traub, Bonhoeffer spoke "calmly, smoking his cigarette, as if he was not saying anyting special: I know what I have chosen."[18] Thus, a witness substantiates the inference that it was 1939 when Bonhoeffer self-consciously chose to enter the political resistance.

The date is important for understanding the ethic of discipleship, for, in the main, commentators have placed Bonhoeffer's entrance into the political resistance somewhat later and so introduced a gap between it and the period of discipleship (which has made the status of *The Cost of Discipleship* in Bonhoeffer's biography all the more perplexing). I am suggesting here an essential continuity between the "discipleship" and "resistance" phases. Specifically, I am asserting that the conflict with authority—born in his relationship with his father, harnessed in the ethic of discipleship through the paradox of obedience, and manifested as the guide leading the disciple into contact with reality—reached its zenith in the period of political resistance. Only in one fairly superficial sense was this phase a negation of discipleship. More profoundly, it was the re-enactment of the disciple's most primeval and paradoxical motives. Political resistance fulfilled discipleship by providing a forum for the paradoxes to be enacted and thereby robbing them of some of their force. Only after the period of political resistance, during Bonhoeffer's imprisonment, did he go beyond discipleship.

The biographical evidence for my assertion is fairly clear. Its essence is that Bonhoeffer is here shown to have allied himself with the political conspiracy within a year and a half after the publication of *The Cost of Discipleship* and less than a year after writing *Life Together*, though before he began his attempts to write *Ethics* and a full five years before he himself questioned his book on discipleship. To be sure, while writing *The Cost of Discipleship* Bonhoeffer was not committed to political resistance per se but, rather, to the church struggle. But that datum is beside the point, for, following Bethge, we have observed that the central features of discipleship were present in Bonhoeffer's thought prior to the 1933 victory of National Socialism, so no argument has been advanced here that discipleship was shaped in response to the church struggle. The point I am asserting is that Bonhoeffer's political activities were related to the same constellation of forces that shaped the ethic of discipleship. What must be done in order to understand this relationship is to explain, psychologically, why Bonhoeffer was no sooner on the boat to America in 1939 than he wrote in his diary, "I am quite clear that I must go back."[19] Then we will be in a position to appreciate the motives (and the conflict of loyalties) that led Bonhoeffer along a path of political resistance that constituted the culminating paradoxical enactment of discipleship. My thesis is that obedience to his father, together with the opportunity that obedience provided for him to prove himself in the family arena, was the impulse leading both to the formulation of discipleship and ultimately to his return to Germany.

But let us begin not with the private but with the public reasons for Bonhoeffer's return. Having set sail for the United States on 4 June 1939, he wrote in July to one of his sponsors, Reinhold Niebuhr, informing him of his decision to return to Germany. In an often-quoted passage, these are the reasons Bonhoeffer gave: "I must live through this difficult period of our national history with the Christian people of Germany. I will have no right to participate in the reconstruction of Christian life in Germany after the war if I do not share the trials of this time with my people."[20] The sentiments are noble, but already we can read between the lines and find in them motives not typically discerned. To begin with, he writes of returning to "live through this difficult period . . . with the Christian people of Germany" and "sharing the trials of this time with my people." Not an outright lie, but the truth is stretched, for Bonhoeffer was returning to no stable pastorate in Germany, no post in theology, indeed to very little Christian fellowship. His "people," those he was returning to, were mostly the non-Christians of his family. To be sure, once Bonhoeffer had committed himself to the conspiracy, he also resigned himself to the prospect of never again serving the church in an official capacity; for reasons of conscience, even he thought political conspiracy and the ministry could not co-exist. Thus, since he knew quite well that his return to Germany would be a return to his family, and also that his family was engaged in political resistance, he surely knew that he was not returning to the "Christian people" as he told Niebuhr. Second, he writes that he "will have no right to participate in the reconstruction of Christian life in Germany" if he does not return. What kind of logic is this? On one hand, had not Bonhoeffer done enough for the cause of Christianity under the Third Reich—arguably more than any other German theologian—to participate in its reconstruction after the war? Surely he had, and this excessive moral zeal must have its roots elsewhere. On the other hand, by what logic does Bonhoeffer argue that only a return to Germany will allow him to participate in the reconstruction of the German church after the war. He must have known that a return to Germany would implicate him in the political conspiracy and thus actually *prohibit* him from formal involvement in Christian life after the war. To be sure, in July of 1939 he could not foresee all the events that would unfold for him, but he certainly had an inkling of them, and this inkling alone makes his explanation to Niebuhr nonsense. We can only make sense of this if we understand Bonhoeffer to be saying that it is in the eyes of his family, not of his church, that he will have no rights if he remains in exile through the war. It is to his family that he must prove his Christian mettle. He had already done so to his church, and a return to Germany would demolish, not strengthen, that proof. More than even he knew, Bonhoeffer's letter to Neibuhr revealed other than Christian motives for his declining his American invitations.

I say that Bonhoeffer himself did not know his true motivation. This is shown by his writings of the time. In his diary he reports: "It is remarkable how I am never quite clear about the motives for any of my decisions. Is that a sign of confusion, of inner dishonesty, or is it a sign that we are guided without our knowing, or is it both?"[21] Or again: "One can give a reason for everything. In the last resort one acts from a level which remains hidden from us."[22] Thus, if Bonhoeffer was "quite clear" that he must return to Germany in 1939, he himself was baffled by the reasons. Even he doubted the reasons he gave Niebuhr. While he was undoubtedly a Christian committed to his country and his church, these reasons alone were not sufficient even for Dietrich Bonhoeffer to justify his return. In consequence, he spent several agitated weeks in New York, complaining about the music and the language (which had caused him little difficulty in either his 1930–31 stay in New York or in his 1934–35 stay in London), tormented by a script that had been written for him when he first committed himself to theology and exacerbated by the unchosen historical challenge. Then, when his decision to return was firm, he reflected in his diary that his greatest regret regarding it was for Sabine (while the refugees who needed a pastor and the American churches who needed information and inspiration went unmentioned). It was only Sabine, forced into exile, who could not be present in Berlin when Bonhoeffer set out to fulfill the life plan that he and his family had set for him.

Thus it was that the ethic of discipleship, forged in a family context, was finally completed in that same context. For when Bonhoeffer joined his family in political resistance, it was the first time in his life that he had stood as a peer and an equal to his father and brothers. In joining them in resistance he was, on one hand, obeying them. But, on the other hand, he was effecting his life plan to prove to them the value of faith. If he had to accept them for the first time as equals and co-workers, and not opponents, they, too, had to accept him on his own terms. Moreover, in the resistance the other elements of Bonhoeffer's earliest ethical impulses were also present. Standing in quasi-identification with his dead brother Walter, he also might risk a wartime death. But his death, unlike Walter's, would be the death of one who fights against war, not in a war. Furthermore, he risked his life in the hope that it would preserve the national community which the Bonhoeffers considered their special heritage to preserve. Thus the constellation of events in the resistance paralleled those in the Bonhoeffer family of 1918 and allowed Dietrich to re-enact that primal drama—this time to break free of it.

Surely it is this psychological sense of discipleship, relating the near-pacifist disciple with the political conspirator, that accounts for the tendency of contemporaries to take "discipleship" as a catchword for Christian political action. Logically the two are related only paradoxically; psychologically their relationship is firm. Perhaps, too, it is the similarity of psychological issues felt by contemporaries to those experienced in particularly keen ways by Bonhoeffer that help account for the continuing resonance of the ethic of discipleship with contemporary sensibilities. These issues—the fragmentation of social (and family) solidarity, the concomitant collapse of authority, the ascendancy of instrumental reason, the search for a kind of spiritual authenticity that will lodge responsibly in the political community—are live dilemmas in our civilization, as they were especially tormenting to Bonhoeffer. But Bonhoeffer, as I have said, did not remain with the answers that the ethic of discipleship provided to these dilemmas. He went beyond that ethic. By way of conclusion, let us turn to a consideration of this final phase in Bonhoeffer's life in an attempt to appreciate the triumph of discipleship: that Bonhoeffer was able to transcend it and its psychological antecedents and to broach a political theory and theology for a religionless, totalitarian age.

V

Conclusion: The Triumph of Discipleship

Narcissus has taunted western civilization from its inception.[1] Today, the challenge of Narcissus is posed most directly by the discipline of psychology. At issue is the relationship between self-absorption—even self-love—and the bonds of community. Psychology, by reason of its perspective, implicitly supposes that what is most important is what goes on in the interior life of the individual, and it tacitly relegates to secondary importance the life of the community. Such has not always been the case. Aristotle, for example, included his discussion of the emotions in his work on rhetoric, not in his work on psychology, and his discussion of the family he placed in *Politics*, not in a separate work on "family psychology" as might be done today. Even Freud and many in the first gen-eration of psychoanalysts, such as Erich Fromm and Erik Erikson, maintained a commitment to civilizational analysis, though it was colored by psychological perceptions. But the contemporary psy-chological *Weltanschauung* has all but abdicated its communal responsibilities. Rather than using the quest for inner authenticity as a point of departure for reflection on problems of authority, the psychological-narcissistic mood of today has chosen to ignore the problem of authority or, worse, to continue to beat its dead corpse.

There was a time when enlightenment, psychological or other-wise, demanded a critique of authority in light of authenticity. But that was a time when the moral fiber of the west was both firm and oppressive. Today, it is the rare situation in which oppression comes by way of authority. The peculiar character of present-day oppression is that it rarely wears the mask of authoritarianism. Instead, it parades as reality itself, the reality of political, economic, or interpersonal power. But the reality of power has always been what authority sets out to legitimize—meaning more than to cloak with legitimations, meaning also to harness and control by means of a political-ethical theory. When psychology—or a psychologi-cally oriented cultural ethos—focuses on the inner life of the individual at the expense of considering the relations among indi-viduals and groups, with an eye to the legitimations of power, it exacerbates the subordination of all to the terror of sheer power. Psychology, like any human study, must take the problem of power to be paramount. In times when power is wielded by an unjust authority, the task of psychology is to criticize this authoritarian-ism. But, in times when authority has collapsed, the task of psy-chology is to lend its hand at constructing a new and just authority. Either way, the analysis of power, whether psychological or other-wise, is always and only a means to an end, the end being the establishing and maintaining of a community in which justice reigns.

Family studies, which should have been able to avoid the mistakes of psychology (thanks to such studies' inherently sociological nature), have proven no better than psychology on these matters. What makes the perspectives of family studies today so potentially devastating is that they have employed the language of politics without appreciating the distinctions among the political, the nonpolitical, and the prepolitical. To Aristotle, the family was neither political nor nonpolitical but, rather, was prepolitical. As a human association it had certain political aspects but, because its main activities centered around the recurrent needs of human beings (productive rationality) rather than the higher, more enduring achievements of humankind, it was but a prepolitical prototype of the kind of association in which humankind's greatest happiness might be attained, the polis. To this prepolitical understanding of the family, the New England Puritans added a prereligious understanding. God chose, they thought, "to lay the foundations both of State and Church, in a family, making that the Mother Hive, out of which both those swarms of State and Church issued forth."[2] But today one rarely hears a family scholar talking about the *pre*political or *pre*religious status of the family. Instead, one hears phrases like "sexual politics" or "politics of experience," and finds family scholars uncritically equating family power with patriarchal authoritarianism with family violence. The language is robbed from political discourse, creating the inescapable impression that family scholars see no difference between family and polity. And this union of politics and family life dovetails with the psychologically oriented propensity to acclaim inner truth as authentic and ontologically primary over the "imposed," "artificial" "conventions" of "society." To be sure, we cannot help but feel a certain sympathy for this propensity when it is remembered that our public community is now dominated by that which Aristotle relegated to the household—economics. Still, the question arises: are we not the poorer in failing to distinguish between family and polity—even if we rightly acknowledge the family as a prepolitical arena? Worse, are we not wrong?

The conclusion of a psychological interpretation of the ethic of discipleship is an ideal place to raise these questions. For throughout this essay I have stressed two things about Bonhoeffer's ethic of discipleship that have direct bearing on these larger theoretical questions. First, I have suggested that the ethic of discipleship was not a static thing that Bonhoeffer erected and embraced unequivocally, but, rather, that it was his kind of experiment with truth that grew alongside him and that he ultimately outgrew and discarded. What has not been systematically developed is my argument for why I think this was the theoretical case. This argument is intimately related to the dialectic of authenticity and authority. In the main, my argument asserts that, when the quest is for authenticity, the experiential correlate of this search is the maternal relationship. And, to embellish a motif in Hannah Arendt's political philosophy as well as a puzzle in Aristotle's portrait of the family (wherein the "natural desire to leave behind them an image of themselves" seems to be a huge exception to the cyclical nature of family life[3]), my hunch that this search may lead to creative liberation is tied to the fact of natality—the province of the woman and not the man—the capacity to begin. This argument will be developed in part by contrasting Bonhoeffer's ethic of discipleship with the sociopsychological portraits of other religious ethics born in paternal rebellion and therefore fixed in either affirmation or negation of the prevailing social structure.

The second theme of my argument is that the significance of the ethic of discipleship, although born in a family context and carried in the psychological constitution of Bonhoeffer, is not sociopsychological but political and religious. Again, the justification for psychological interpretation is not merely to show how a political or religious complex can be traced to a psychological context. That everybody knows already, even if one does not know the precise contours of the psychological outline. Rather, the challenge of a psychological interpretation is to show how the ideas developed in a psychological context later lodged in a nonpsychological context. It is with this challenge in mind that later pages attempt to extrapolate from the ethic of discipleship the political (and to some extent religious) critique contained, at least in embryonic form, in it. Specifically, in the second and third sections of this chapter I want to turn from the psychological orientation that has dominated my study thus far and consider the political theory nestled within the ethic of discipleship. Far from being a negation of my thesis, this reorientation represents its culmination, for it is the public and not the private life of Bonhoeffer that remains significant today. A final section will briefly speculate on this public significance. But let us now turn to the first task: considering the status of Bonhoeffer and the ethic of discipleship in the psychological study of religious ethics.

Authority and the Ethic of Discipleship

The theoretical significance of my study of Bonhoeffer must be assessed by counterpoising its interpretations with the prevailing views and issues in the social psychology of religious ethics and ethicists. Few would argue with the general assertion that the prevailing views are those established by psychoanalysis, particularly the ego psychology of Erik Erikson, especially as his ideas are embedded in his seminal work, *Young Man Luther*.[4] Indeed, although all previous psychological studies of Bonhoeffer are by no means squarely in this tradition, one essay is straightforward in its stated attempt to study "Bonhoeffer in the context of Erikson's Luther study."[5] Moreover, it is probably fair to say that even those which are less overtly aligned with psychoanalysis are, nevertheless, implicitly indebted to the paradigm generated by Freud and later Erikson. No responsible psychological work on a religious ethicist can avoid acquaintance with Erikson and, as a result, dialogue with psychoanalysis.

Under these circumstances, it is well to begin the present theoretical discussion by noting the near-universal theme of all studies of this genre: rebellion against an authoritarian father. This, of course, is the theme of Freud's classic exercise in metapsychology, *Totem and Taboo*, as it is also the central theme of Erikson's *Young Man Luther* which finds Luther's development to be an "almost exclusively masculine affair." Psychological interpretations of Bonhoeffer generally see him through the lenses of paternal influences and expectations, and the social psychology of religion generally has found it hard to resist the manifest structural parallel between God the Father and the real father of one's childhood. According to this theory, again most eloquently stated in Erikson's monograph on Luther, through rebellion against a real and then surrogate and then symbolic father, the soon-to-be religious leader hits a kind of "rock bottom"—a "negative identity"—from which he can fashion a startlingly new ethic which "re-evaluates the premises of his society." And, lest the facts be misrepresented, it is clear that Bonhoeffer enacted a struggle with his father which, in broad sweeps, is described by this theory.

But the centrality of the father/son relationship in these theories recalls the patriarchal-bourgeois family type that prevailed in Freud's and Luther's day. Moreover, it recalls a time when social and familial life evidenced sufficient moral stability to grant the patriarch legitimacy and so to understand his power as authority.

The story has been different in this century, for this century has seen the bifurcation of authority into power and nihilism, and it is upon this unstable soil that specifically modern tyranny— totalitarianism—and the modern family grow. Indeed, just as political theorists have questioned "authoritarianism" as the apt designation for totalitarianism, so also family scholars must come to see that it is precisely the absence of authority that constitutes the point of departure for the modern family. So again: if it is clear that Bonhoeffer enacted a struggle with his father, it is equally clear that the description of this struggle alone does not exhaust a psychological interpretation of his development. It is often his flight from this struggle, from the threat of tyranny and the fragmented communal solidarity underlying it, rather than authoritarianism that enables us to understand Bonhoeffer. In other words, and in an idea that will be picked up in a moment, Bonhoeffer's mother had much to do with his religious and ethical development.

Before considering the maternal influences on Bonhoeffer, however, we should appreciate the root sociological issue underlying the psychological one. It is simply that, unlike Luther, when Bonhoeffer "rebelled," *there was no "rock bottom" to "hit."* It is the nature of the totalitarian society in which he lived that rebellion was no more salient than the authoritarianism against which it was directed, for beneath both lurked not a rock bottom, but only a kind of void or abyss—terms which Bonhoeffer used several times to describe his society in his *Ethics*. Under such conditions there is no point of leverage; the critic becomes only the crank, the rebel only the vandal. Where authority wanes, those who propose to fight it find that its shell cracks easily and they are left floundering in meaningless rebellion, becoming a part of the very structures they sought to shatter. Bonhoeffer well understood this dilemma of his times. Circling around it in *Ethics*, he put his thumb directly on it in his privately circulated essay for the conspirators, "After Ten Years." There he wrote: "One may ask whether there

have ever before in human history been people with so little
ground under their feet—people to whom every available alternative seemed equally intolerable, repugnant, and futile, who
looked beyond all these existing alternatives for the source of
their strength."[6] Here Bonhoeffer, the moral voice of the conspiracy, their pastor, can suggest no moral vision. Instead, he can
only suggest that there is another, albeit unmentioned, source of
strength. And it is with my noting of the dimension of ground-
lessness, rootlessness, even nihilism, that the present study departs
from previous ones. Specifically, I find the father/son complex a
difficult anchorage for a dilemma that transcends all existing alternatives and searches for a new source of strength.

With this sociological insight we must turn from Erikson's study
of Luther to his less well-known study of Gandhi. For, if Erikson
considered Luther's development to have been an "almost exclusively masculine affair," that view was not an essential tenet to
psychological analysis as he perceived it, since about Gandhi he
asserted: "in order to have the courage to surpass his father [Gan-
dhi] . . . had to strive to become a new kind of leader in whom
paternal and maternal identifications coincide."[7] Enter the potential significance of the mother, even to psychoanalysis. But along
with Erikson's Gandhi, another religious ethicist should be considered: Augustine. It is not paternal rebellion that pervades
Augustine's *Confessions*, but it was to his mother that the saint
looked for experiential assistance in nurturing an embryonic religious ethic. Unlike Luther and more like Bonhoeffer, Augustine
cared not to hit, through rebellion, some rock bottom on which
to build; his search was for the "intrinsic order of being, reality,
and value"[8]—a search defined on the first page of the *Confessions*:
"You have made us for yourself, and our hearts are restless until
they rest in you." Bonhoeffer's similar ontological search has been
stressed by interpreters, and the insistence here is that, like Augustine, he employed a close relationship with his mother as an

experiential correlate of his spiritual journey. Indeed, it is revealing to reflect briefly on the marked difference between Bonhoeffer's and Luther's spiritual quests. Luther, it will be
remembered, agonized over the fate of his soul, and it was only
in the resolution of this agony through faith that his ethic was
born. By contrast, Bonhoeffer first dismissed the question of personal salvation in discipleship by arguing for a praxic, socially
committed religiosity, and later he dismissed the question altogether as unbiblical. Rather, for Bonhoeffer "the most important
question . . . is how we can find a basis for human life together,
what spiritual realities and laws we accept as the foundation of a
meaningful human life"[9] Of course, these religious differences
are isomorphic with the psychological differences between the
two ethicists: Luther, in rebellion against his father, found guilt to
be the impelling motive for faith; Bonhoeffer, in alliance with his
mother, found broken community and its psychological corollary,
shame, to be the impetus for faith. In terms of the social psychology of religious ethicists, then, Bonhoeffer finds more fellowship with Gandhi and Augustine than with Luther.

   None of this is intended to imply that for Bonhoeffer—or for
Augustine or Gandhi for that matter—it was his mother who contributed "more" to his development than his father; it is never so
simple a matter as that. Rather, the intention is to suggest strict,
if general, parallels between types of social, political, religious,
and familial challenges and their relations one to another. In the
world in which Bonhoeffer lived, a world to which we are the
direct heirs, the issue of authoritarianism is not paramount. In
religion, his and ours, issues revolve not so much around the
authority of God as around the character of the community that
is rightly called God's dominion. In the family, the issue is no
longer patriarchal authoritarianism but is now a kind of paternal
tyranny made possible by the anomie tht has accompanied the
erosion of familial solidarity and its replacement by an emotional

calculus of technical reason. In society and politics, issues no longer center on authoritarian domination; rather, they center on the incipient and ultimately nihilistic domination by technique. Under these conditions, the threat is no longer authoritarian oppression but, rather, the danger that the search for "authenticity" will find no ground and thus will degenerate into instrumentality or even violence. In this world, then, the task is to fashion from the outmoded structures of the old world a new basis of life together. When the challenge is of this kind—to transcend rebellion and to create a meaningful foundation for social life—the guiding figure is not the male, but that figure who brings forth nascent life: the female.

It remains only to direct these theoretical considerations to the final and most enigmatic phase of Bonhoeffer's life: the period of "religionless Christianity" which has here been associated with personal, psychological liberation. Some truly great ethicists, like Luther, seemingly never achieved this stage of freedom but remained ensnared by the ethical web of their own construction. How do we know that Bonhoeffer transcended the ethic of discipleship? Mostly we learn it from his own pen, for in *Letters and Papers from Prison*, in the same months that he inaugurates his program of religionless Christianity, he writes of discipleship as the end of a path and, elsewhere, of his life as making sense till then though also being a thorough preparation for a new beginning. In addition we can infer the transcendence in various other ways. For one, the metaphor *Mündigkeit*, with which he characterizes the world come of age, is drawn from developmental imagery, referring to the age at which a child becomes an adult. For another, there is the fact that only in 1943 did he become engaged to be married, suggesting that he no longer felt the need to heed the disciple's inner call for celibacy. Indeed, the ground on which he broke off his relationship with a girlfriend eight years earlier was that the times were too dangerous for marriage—yet surely the danger was much greater in 1943. And there are more subtle indicators of personal liberation in *Letters and Papers from Prison*. For example, in one of them he writes that he has finally "got over the dangers of psychology" and is "very interested in it again."[10] On one level, this comment probably indicates that he has become better acquainted and less afraid of his own psychological makeup. On another level, it probably attests to an easier relationship with his father, the psychiatrist. Similarly, Bonhoeffer writes frankly of his former irrational dismissal of the natural sciences and laments that he never studied them, perhaps also an indication of a relaxation of the conflict between his religious mother and scientific father. Finally, Bonhoeffer's altered attitude toward death, which will be discussed in the final section of this chapter, also suggests personal liberation.

How was Bonhoeffer enabled to achieve this liberation? To begin with, what Erikson dubs "the curse"—"an aspect of childhood or youth which comes to represent an account that can never be settled and remains an existential debt all the rest of a lifetime"[11]—was indeed settled by Bonhoeffer. Concretely, in the experience of political conspiracy a constellation of familial forces similar to those that first placed the curse on him in 1918 enabled him to reenact the events and overcome them. Rarely do life circumstances permit such a direct re-enactment, but history provided the circumstances for Bonhoeffer and the ethic of discipleship poised him to cope with them. But more to the point, Bonhoeffer would never have broken free of his curse had his father and not his mother been the principal player. The reason is that (insofar as the father is representative of the world outside the home) the father/son complex permits only conforming submission or rebellious negation. To break free of a curse, one must transcend both affirmation and negation. For this transcendence, again, the experiential correlate is typically the mother, who represents as-yet-unknown potentialities rather than established actualities to the child.

Ultimately, of course, this process of psychological liberation is shrouded in mystery. How a re-enactment breaks psychological chains, the mystery of psychological cure from Freud onward, is inexplicable. To complicate the matter, as often as not, the re-enactment simply repeats the original failure and solidifies rather than removes the curse. In the last analysis, therefore, liberation must be seen to be premised not only on re-enactment but also on a certain talent and struggle on the part of the actor who, the second time around, manages to get things right. Again, the corollary to this ability is the maternal relationship, which first instills in the child the sense of trust in his or her own abilities. Even so, such trust is but a prerequisite. In the end, the mystery of liberation is nothing less than the miracle of life itself: the ability to act, to create, to begin and begin again. It is this ability that enables Bonhoeffer's legacy, begun in the ethic of discipleship, to live on—not as a static, authoritarian ethic but as a dynamic critique. Let us turn to the political critique that began to emerge in *The Cost of Discipleship* and grew increasingly pointed thereafter.

The Critique of Tyranny

Nazism, as was suggested in Chapter I, was not simply political authoritarianism run rampant. More fundamentally, it represented a bifurcation of authority. Power was severed from its roots in a theory of justice and became rank tyranny. The leadership principle demonstrated this: power was based only upon the will of the *Führer*, nothing more. Law, politics, parties, justice—all—were obsolete. What mattered was power, a power that dominated so completely as to destroy its subordinate. There was no rule other than "might makes right," no legitimations beyond deference to the tyrant's will. This rule was not authoritarianism, for it neither had nor sought any basis in tradition or morality other than the fact of its existence. Scrutinized carefully, it might not even merit the designation *tyranny*, for even the tyrant rules for perverted pleasure or despotic plunder—yet Hitler and his henchmen seemed bent only on the most nihilistic aim that power can will: destruction. Hitler, who had once been an itinerant poster-painter and concocted some of the most magnificent architectural schemes ever envisoned for Europe, seemed somewhere to have exchanged his impulse to create with a rage to destroy. An antiauthoritarian, Hitler made even a poor tyrant: indifferent to plunder and unformidable as a gangster. Bent solely on power for power's sake, a motive that can be manifested only in destruction, men like Hitler were described by Bonhoeffer as "petty tyrants."

This examination of tyranny is not to suggest that Bonhoeffer, consciously or unconsciously, perceived his father to be a tyrant. Little could be more misleading than to make such an accusation. All the same, there were tyrannical aspects to the relationship between father and son. Partly these were born as a result of the father's personality, which was probably more like his son's than he cared to admit. Masking his sensitivity behind a perhaps overly disciplined facade, Karl Bonhoeffer, too, had his own ambivalence toward power. The reason we have seen little of this ambivalence in the senior Bonhoeffer is, simply, that almost every time we have seen him, he has been in control and his authority has been unquestioned. Indeed, when his authority was questioned—by the Nazi regime—he reacted instantly and violently. Karl Bonhoeffer had shades of egotism, even tyranny, that pitted him sometimes against a son with similar dispositions. But this is not the main point to be made here. The main point is a theoretical one. It is that the legitimate authority of Karl Bonhoeffer was only as strong as the communal solidarity in which it was embedded. Ergo, in the eyes of the twelve-year-old Dietrich when he feared the loss of his familial solidarity through the withdrawal of his mother, Karl Bonhoeffer's authority was illegitimate: it was tyranny. Again, this is the theoretical nature of the case: authority can be sustained only by a community, otherwise it ipso facto becomes tyranny. But the family crisis was exacerbated in Bonhoeffer's eyes by a father who persisted in holding in disdain that which pulled the family back together: religious faith. As a result, Bonhoeffer's lifelong concern with Christian community, rooted in his concern over his own family's community, sensitized him to the problem of tyranny. Indeed, as will be shown below, Bonhoeffer himself was a lifelong authoritarian. It was tyranny that revolted him. Hence it was the fearful suspicion that his father's authority would become tyranny that caused him to fashion his paradox of obedience, and it was the reality of Nazi tyranny that enabled him to provide a trenchant critique of it.

Let us look more closely at Bonhoeffer's thinking about authority, power, and tyranny. Here is seen his trenchant religious critique of totalitarianism. Recalling the paradox of obedience in *The Cost of Discipleship*—"only he who believes is obedient, and only he who is obedient believes"—we see clearly that this is an authoritarian pronouncement. Man is radically subordinated to an unquestioned authoritarian God. In passages that might make certain psychoanalysts recoil, Bonhoeffer is not above writing of man's "absolute insecurity" in the face of God's "absolute authority,"[12] or of faith as "passive submission."[13] So deep is this religious authoritarianism that it sometimes shades into rank elitism, as in this passage from *Ethics*:

> Everything that we have said about responsibility can in the end apply only to a small group of men.... For the great majority of men one must speak not of responsibility

but of obedience and duty. This implies one ethic for the great and the strong, for the rulers, and another for the small and the weak, the subordinates; on the one hand responsibilitiy and on the other obedience, on the one hand freedom and on the other subservience. . . . [I]t is granted to only a very few men to breathe the free air of the wide open spaces of great decisions and to experience the hazard of responsible action which is entirely their own.[14]

Bonhoeffer struggles with the moral dilemma of a pastor involved in political resistance, and his authoritarianism shades easily into aristocratic elitism. Indeed, as passages like this one suggest, when Bonhoeffer writes of submission and similar ideas, he means them in the quite ordinary sense of one person being subordinated to another whose authority is greater—the ultimate authority, of course, being God known through Jesus Christ.

From the very beginning it was upon this basis of religious authoritarianism that Bonhoeffer leveled his critique of the "leadership principle." In his radio talk and speech of 1933, for example, he exclaimed: "The fearful danger of the present time is that above the cry for authority . . . we forget that man stands alone before the ultimate authority."[15] Thus it was not on antiauthoritarian grounds that Bonhoeffer opposed fascism, but on the grounds of religious authoritarianism. The problem with the *Führer* was not that he was authoritarian, but that he was a tyrant who usurped God's rightful authority and elevated the state to a position that encroached upon the authority of the church. Indeed, the first half-decade of Bonhoeffer's opposition to national Socialism was not first a political opposition to the Reich but a religious defense of the church that had its authority robbed from it by a tyrannical state. Elsewhere in his *Ethics* he even shrouds his political involvement in a subtle manipulation of Luther's two kingdoms doctrine.

Introducing a distinction between "state" and "government," he argues that the state is a fundamentally eschatological concept referring to the future city of God and that only the relatively mundane business of government is a biblically mandated order—and a "penultimate" one at that, subject always to the "ultimate" authority of the word of God.[16] From its inception, Bonhoeffer's critique of totalitarianism was erected upon authoritarian grounds.

But if Bonhoeffer indicted Nazism from a posture of religious authoritarianism, did he perceive Nazism as tyranny in the sense discussed here? The answer, already anticipated by noting his phrase "petty tyrant," is yes. But to discover it we must dig in a dark corner, for nothing of substance remains of Bonhoeffer's writings that directly indicts National Socialism—if indeed he was foolish enough to write such material. The political situation was simply too dangerous for a man like Bonhoeffer to write even unpublished pieces attacking the Reich directly. Consequently, for Bonhoeffer's critique of Nazi tyranny we must look at indirect sources, and these sources are readily available in his fictional writings. There during his first year of imprisonment, he allowed himself to reflect upon the horror of totalitarianism in the kind of oblique way in which writers of fiction make political points. It is here that we find his critique of "petty tyranny."

Since we are prepared for what will be discovered in Bonhoeffer's fiction, a question raised by a commentator on it will not seem as striking as it otherwise might, but it is well to begin the present discussion with that question. Although he "was surrounded with so many acts of gross evil and inhumanity in Nazi Germany," why did Bonhoeffer focus on "comparatively minor instances of evil"?[17] The query refers to two of Bonhoeffer's stories, both of which deal with relatively unpowerful bullies. Bonhoeffer calls them "petty tyrants" and answers the interpreter's question this way:

It is petty tyrants who destroy a nation at its core; they are the tubercular bacteria which secretly destroy a flourishing young life. They are not only more dangerous but also stronger, tougher, harder to get hold of than the big ones. They slip through your fingers when you want to grab them, for they are smooth and cowardly. They are like a contagious disease. When such a tyrant sucks the vital strength from his victim he simultaneously infects him with his spirit; and as soon as this tyrant's victim gets hold of the least bit of power himself, he takes revenge for what has happened to him. But this revenge—this is the horror—is not directed against the guilty, but against the innocent, defenseless victims. And so it goes endlessly, until at last all is infected and poisoned and dissolution can no longer be stopped.[18]

To an authoritarian, who by definition affirms the values of sociality in which legitimacy is created and maintained, the root evil of totalitarian leaders is precisely their smallness, their pettiness, their tyrannical rather than authoritarian rule. Indeed, far from baffling, this passage shows Bonhoeffer to have a profound grasp of the social psychology of totalitarian leadership. Its irony lies in its pettiness, yet it is the pettiness that is the most horrid of all: for it is the very pettiness of the totalitarian tyrant that causes him to turn his wrath not on the deserving but on the helpless. Were he authoritarian, his domination would at least be directed by a modicum of socially shared rationality. As a petty tyrant, his only rationality is of weakness and strength. It is because of this feature of totalitarian domination that discipleship's paradox of obedience found a political foothold.

Thus it is that Bonhoeffer's own personal struggle with authority and tyranny, crystallized in the ethic of discipleship's paradox of obedience, traveled from the prepolitical family arena in which it was born to the political arena proper. It is also interesting to note the route it traveled. If it was present, essentially as Christian authoritarianism, in 1933, it was only toward the conclusion of the discipleship phase, in the drafts of *Ethics* and then in his prison fiction, that it increasingly became a self-conscious political critique. This trail from the family to the church and politics is also discernible in Bonhoeffer's critique of instrumental reason, nestled in discipleship as the paradox of costly grace and—also like his critique of tyranny—premised on a commitment to sociality.

The Critique of Instrumental Reason

Psychologically, the costliness of grace had a fairly specific meaning for the architect of discipleship. The cost of grace was rooted in the fact of mortality and the social disintegration that death brings to a community. From that basis, one can trace the emergence of this construct in Bonhoeffer's life and thought. But, as with the paradox of obedience that had biographical moorings but political implications for Nazi tyranny, so also costly grace struck at the core of the social structure that enabled totalitarianism to emerge. The bifurcation of authority at the century's turn, after all, had tyranny as only one of its manifestations. The other manifestation was a nihilism that had become historically concrete in the guise of instrumental rationality. For tyranny to become totalitarianism, what is required is not only the tyrant but also the technological infrastructure and bureaucratic social structure that enables destruction to become a problem of administration. Victims of totalitarianism, unlike victims of tyranny, are defined completely "objectively" and their massacre is correspondingly an "objective" problem of administration and technological development. Such victims, defined objectively and exterminated bureaucratically, are not even allowed graves. This kind of totalitarian domination requires men who themselves are not tyrants but who are so thoroughly instrumental in their moral orientation that they can execute the tyrant's will with considerable expertise and complete moral indifference. Such a man is described in Arendt in her portrayal of Eichmann. Not a tyrant but (as psychiatrists certified and Arendt explicated) "terrifyingly normal," Eichmann was the "Nazi expert" on the "Jewish question." Never himself guilty of harming a Jew, and even personally fond of the race and a Zionist, Eichmann nevertheless supervised the transport of millions of Jews to their deaths. Arendt asserts that Eichmann

> did not enter the Party out of conviction, nor was he ever convinced by it—whenever he was asked to give his reasons, he repeated the same embarrassed clichés about the Treaty of Versailles and unemployment; rather, as he pointed out in court, "it was like being swallowed up by the Party against all expectations and without previous decision. It happened so quickly and suddenly." He had no time and less desire to be properly informed, he did not even know the Party program, he never read *Mein Kampf*. Kaltenbrunner had said to him: Why not join the S.S.? And he had replied, Why not? That was how it happened, and that was about all there was to it.[19]

Just as Hitler exemplifies the modern tyrant, so Eichmann exemplifies the administrator without whom tyranny could not become totalitarianism. It is this role of administrator or, more precisely, the mode of instrumental reasoning that enables the administrator to arise in contemporary societies, that constitutes the second prong of totalitarianism begging for critique. And it was this second prong of totalitarianism that Bonhoeffer implicitly shattered with his metaphor of costly grace. For the metaphor of costly grace was set up to shatter technical reasoning in the theological sphere. It indicts both the Nazi cheap religiosity (*Gottgläubiger*) and the political-theological speculations of the "German Christians" who attempted to legitimate the Reich through a theology of the "orders of creation." Not incidentally, it was *Gottgläubiger* that Eichmann claimed as his religious identity to the end of his life—a Nazi-sanctioned vague belief in God, but neither a moral God nor a God of salvation. To the Bonhoeffer of costly grace, however, God could neither be subjectivized into an irrelevant private belief nor objectivized into a legitimator for orders of creation; rather, God is both subjective and objective, and nothing can be deduced from grace other than the praxis of obedience and faith. In the sociopolitical sphere, therefore, costly grace implicitly condemns any disjunction between the instrumental and the ethical.

As we have seen, the metaphor of costly grace was a relatively late addition to Bonhoeffer's work on discipleship. It seems that it was the paradox of obedience that dominated Bonhoeffer's concerns during the middle 1930s, and only upon the final writing of *The Cost of Discipleship* did he decide to begin his exposition of the Christian life with this metaphor. Yet we have seen that the placing of this last-minute addition in the front of the manuscript is true to its biographical importance. It was, indeed, the problem of community and its polyphonic bases that first inspired the young Bonhoeffer, and only later did the struggle with tyranny pose itself as a derivative problem. It is as if, in a final and satisfying afterthought, Bonhoeffer decided to set the tone of his treatise on obedience with a metaphor that called forth the central issues of community on which the problem of obedience was erected. Nevertheless, it was the problem of community, and specifically of the instrumental reasoning that undergirded a fragmented community, that embodied the deepest critique Bonhoeffer leveled against totalitarianism. In essence, tyrants may come or go, and so long as social life is sufficiently solid they need pose no dire threat. Similarly, in the Christian life, so long as one responds appropriately to grace, the details of community, faith, and obedience will follow truly. Thus it is no wonder that, although he discussed petty tyranny in his fictional writings, it was the problem of reason and technology that Bonhoeffer chose to tackle directly in his *Ethics*. About reason he writes:

> Reason became a working hypothesis, a heuristic principle, and so led on to the unparalleled rise of technology. This is something essentially new in the history of the world. From the Egyptian pyramids and the Greek temples to the medieval cathedrals and the eighteenth century, technology had always been a matter of artisanship. It stood in the service of religion, of kings, of art, and of the daily needs of men. The technical science of the modern western world has emancipated itself from any kind of subservience. It is in essence not service but mastery.... Technology became an end in itself. It has a soul of its own. Its symbol is the machine.[20]

Thus, for the Bonhoeffer of *Ethics*, the west had witnessed an eclipse of reason which went stage by stage with the rise of modern technology and science. The result was that technology had become no longer a means, but an end. Like a car stuck in the mud, technology had reached its limit in his day.[21] It had because technology brought with it the "atomization of human society" which, "in the name of human equality and human dignity," has made "man himself an abstraction."[22] The final result, Bonhoeffer writes, echoing Nietzsche, is nihilism: "The master of the machine becomes its slave. The machine becomes the enemy of men. The emancipation of the masses leads to the reign of terror of the guillotine. . . . The liberation of man as an abstract ideal leads only to man's self-destruction. At the end of the path which was first trodden in the French Revolution there is nihilism."[23]

In these passages Bonhoeffer's aristocratic conservatism continues to show, and this makes them all the more remarkable. For in them Bonhoeffer propounds a critique of reason and technology—implicitly the foundation of totalitarianism—that developed independently from, and in most cases predates, the critique of his German-Marxist contemporaries. What is surprising is that he developed his critique in complete isolation from them and solely on the basis of his own religious quest—which, as has been shown, was part of his larger biographical quest. As he summarized the world's state: "natural life stands between the extremes of vitalism and mechanization," both of which are "expressions . . . of despair."[24] Here he summarized his biographical challenge, his religious ethic, and his political critique. Biographically he was threatened on two fronts: by the patriarch who threatened tyranny (as well as the ego that threatened itself to tyrannize); and by the familial community that threatened with its own potential fragmentation or, worse, mechanized pseudosolidarity. In his religious ethic he attacked both forms of despair with an authoritarian paradox of obedience and a metaphor of the price of grace.

The enduring significance of Bonhoeffer is that concerns born in his life as personal and religious provided him with the basis for a trenchant if embryonic political critique. On one hand, his concern with the despair of "vitalism" provided the foundation for a critique of the tyranny epitomized by Hitler; on the other hand, his concern with the despair of "mechanization" provided

the foundation for a critique of the instrumental reasoning epitomized by countless living and breathing but nevertheless nihilistic men like Eichmann. Bonhoeffer's concerns, whatever their
biographical roots, can never be limited in importance to idiosyncratic individual psychology, for his critique is ultimately political. Our inheritance of a common political world, rather than
affinities of psychology and disposition, gives Bonhoeffer's thought
its resonance even today with acting men and women.

A New Prophet?

At the outset of this study there was occasion to observe Nietzsche's
prognosis for the twentieth century. He foretold the collapse of
authority and its bifurcation into a dialectic of nihilism and power.
Moreover, we have just seen how the ethic of discipleship contained an embryonic critique of this same dialectic. This perception brings us to a question raised by a student of Nietzsche and
a teacher of Bonhoeffer, Max Weber. Weber, too, understood the
crisis of authority in the west, and he also understood it to be a
dialectic of instrumental rationality and power. At the conclusion
of his *Protestant Ethic and the Spirit of Capitalism*, for example,
he lamented the death of the once-compelling Protestant ethic,
and its replacement by "specialists without spirit, sensualists without heart," a "nullity" that "imagines that it has attained a level of
civilization never before achieved."[25] For Weber this represented
a prison for the west, which he designated as an "iron cage." But,
unlike Nietzsche, Weber did not foreclose the possibility of a
religious response to this crisis. He wrote: "No one knows who
will live in this cage in the future, or whether at the end of this
tremendous development entirely new prophets will arise, or

there will be a great rebirth of old ideas and ideals, or, if neither, mechanized petrification, embellished with a sort of convulsive self-importance."[26] "Mechanized petrification, embellished with a sort of convulsive self-importance" echoes Nietzsche's dialectic of nihilism and power. But what can we make of the hypothesis about the possibility of a new prophet? Could Bonhoeffer be one?

The questions are worth raising because of the tremendous resonance of the ethic of discipleship around the world today and the intrigue of Bonhoeffer to politically-conscious Christians. But, in the main, our response to these questions, although yes in both instances, must distinguish between Bonhoeffer as spokesperson for discipleship and Bonhoeffer's story as such. As spokesperson for discipleship, Bonhoeffer certainly has a claim to prophetic status: witness the attraction of the ethic of discipleship by modern Christians posed with political dilemmas not always unlike those confronting Bonhoeffer. Thus, at least on the level of discernible sociological impact, Bonhoeffer's prophetic status is validated by the continuing resonance of the ethic of discipleship, and Weber's historical prognosis—over Nietzsche's—has found embodiment.

But matters are perhaps not so simple in our century. Nietzsche, after all, was not merely guilty of historical omission when he failed to note the possibility of the emergence of a new prophet; he concluded, rather, that his writing of the first few chapters of the "history of morality" had once and for all established a cultural environment in which a new prophet could not indeed emerge–an environment, that is, in which the death of God was a common existential acknowledgment. Moreover, one wonders with what degree of conviction Weber included a new prophet as a possible prognosis for late capitalism. It is likely that he did not put much personal hope in that alternative; rather, it was probably intro-duced only as a historical possibility of the theoretical sort: pos-sible in principle, but far from probable. In fact, Weber, too, helped to create the kind of cultural environment in which the emergence and reception of a new prophet would be increasingly less likely. After all, the rational methods of even an interpretive sociology exacerbate the tendency toward disenchantment, and Weber himself found the "abysmal contrast" between facts and values to be a barrier of insurmountable proportions.

In the cultural environment created by Nietzsche, Weber, and others of equal or lesser stature, then, the very possibility of the emergence of religious ethics and new prophets is diminished to the historically unthinkable. How could any potential religious prophet withstand even the relatively benign interpretation Weber advanced of Calvinism? And today we have not an occasional iconoclast, but countless thousands of scientifically trained interpreters in whose hands no religious leader is exempt from thorough, rational interpretation. How, in this milieu where charisma is immediately rationalized by courtiers in psychology, sociology, economics and other areas of expertise—often as early as the next morning's newspaper—can a prophetic religious ethic avoid the sterilizations that legions of cultural gatekeepers perform daily?

For this reason the whole story of Bonhoeffer, and not only of Bonhoeffer as the architect of discipleship, invites deeper consideration of his answer to the Nietzschean lament and the Weberian prognosis. For, although Bonhoeffer erected a religious ethic that resonated to his day and ours, he also had the integrity to see the limits of a purely religious ethic and to ask "what Christianity really is, or indeed who Christ really is, for us today." And this question was premised on the observation that "we are now moving towards a completely religionless time; people as they are now simply cannot be religious anymore." That is, he recognized the limitations of his own endeavor, the impossibility of religious ethics in his day. Yet—this is his originality over against all critics of religion—he insisted upon asking, "How can Christ become Lord of the religionless as well?"[27] Or, as he also put it, he wanted to continue thinking "theologically." Such, then, is Bonhoeffer's deeper claim to prophetic status: that in ruthless authenticity he acknowledged the mistakes of his path, but at the same time he never let loose of his ultimate goal of genuine faith. Thus it is that Bonhoeffer is a unique kind of prophet and one especially suited to an age of authenticity rather than authority: the kind of prophet whose mistakes are as instructive as his successes and who encourages us to find faith in the midst of a psychological and political reality that seems bent on denying it. Of importance in the story of Bonhoeffer is, ultimately, his assertion that faith may—indeed must—be found in the midst of the personal and political contexts that appear to deny it.

Nowhere is this prophetic message of Bonhoeffer's stronger than in his attitude toward death. As has been shown in this study, it was death that acted as the catalyst for Bonhoeffer's childhood theological aspirations. It is also a well-known argument that death in general is an impetus for faith among the many Christians who assent to faith in the hope of attaining their own immortality. And, as late as his first circular letter to the Finkenwalde brethren of the war, Bonhoeffer is not above consoling his students who are facing their own deaths with the "comfort" of the "God of the resurrection."[28] But as the war proceeds and Bonhoeffer's own introspection intensifies, he increasingly dismisses a "god of the gaps," a god whose activities begin where human powers leave off, a *deus ex machina*. By 1943, in fact, he has the very opposite view toward death. Then he writes:

> Nothing can make up for the absence of someone whom we love, and it would be wrong to try to find a substitute; we must simply hold out and see it through. This sounds very hard at first, but at the same time it is a great consolation, for the gap, as long as it remains unfilled, preserves the bonds between us. It is nonsense to say that God fills the gap; he doesn't fill it, but on the contrary,

he keeps it empty and so helps us to keep alive our former
communion with each other, even at the cost of pain.[29]

Coupled with his observation that "the individualistic question
about personal salvation [has] almost completely left us all" and
that this change is "in fact biblical,"[30] this passage portrays a unique
man of faith—a man who insists that "before God and with God
we live without God."[31] Hardly the stuff of traditional prophetic
pronouncements, his position is perhaps the only acceptable as
well as edifying religious position palatable to the heirs of Neitzsche.
With it Bonhoeffer changes the ground rules of apologetics. No
longer is discussion centered on the boundary conditions of human
life such as death; rather, the Christian accepts his or her fundamental humanity with the religious and irreligious alike and focuses
dialogue on areas of common concern. For in the last analysis,
according to Bonhoeffer, Jesus is simply "the man for others" and
discipleship—in the broadest sense—means serving others.

In broad sweeps, of course, this motif infuses the ethic of
discipleship, too, and that quality is why when he did distance
himself from it Bonhoeffer still "stood by" what he wrote in *The
Cost of Discipleship*. But the ethic of discipleship, as I have attempted
to show, was really but a specific praxic forum in which Bonhoeffer
waged a psychological, religious, and political battle simultaneously. The specifics of that battle are important not so much for
themselves as for the light they shed on the larger issues they
engage. These issues are primarily those of psychology, political
thought, and religion. Having commented upon what seem to me
to be the psychological and political implications of this battle,
let me venture a comment on its religious significance and the
broadest sense in which Bonhoeffer can be considered a new and
needed prophet.

The ethic of discipleship enabled Bonhoeffer to offer the world
what he had discovered for himself: that God lives not in any

religion, nation, ideology, or scientific theory, but that he is revealed in the midst of humanity, in all its frailties and failures. To be sure, when Bonhoeffer advanced the notion that the world had come of age and was now without religion, he was not blind to the neopaganism that surrounded him in his Fatherland, and neither was he (by then) ignorant of the conditioning arm of his own psychological experience. It was in the face of this disillusionment— no, in the *midst* of it—however, that he continued to sound his prophetic call: that the community in which Christ exists is nothing less than the human community. This ultimate affirmation of the reality of God in the midst of humanity is the abiding legacy of Bonhoeffer's prophetic story.

Notes

CHAPTER I

1. Dietrich Bonhoeffer, *Letters and Papers from Prison*, enlarged ed., trans. Reginald Fuller, Frank Clarke et al., ed. Eberhard Bethge (New York: Macmillan, 1972).

2. Ibid., p. 360.

3. Jacques Ellul, for example, dismisses Bonhoeffer's last writings with this kind of argument in *The New Demons*, trans. C. Edward Hopkins (New York: Seabury Press, 1975).

4. Harvey Cox's *The Secular City* (New York: Macmillan, 1965) is perhaps the most well-known example of this tendency.

5. See Bethge's "Preface of the New Edition" in *Letters and Papers from Prison*.

6. Heinrich Ott, *Reality and Faith: The Theological Legacy of Dietrich Bonhoeffer*, trans. Alex A. Morrison (Philadelphia: Fortress Press, 1972), p. 15.

7. Bonhoeffer, *Letters and Papers from Prison*, p. 275.

8. Dietrich Bonhoeffer, *The Cost of Discipleship*, revised ed., trans. R. H. Fuller with some revisions by Irmgard Booth, foreword by Bishop G. K. A. Bell, Memoir by G. Leibholz (New York: Macmillan, 1963).

9. Bonhoeffer, *Letters and Papers from Prison*, p. 369.

10. One of the two versions of this lecture remains and its English translation, entitled "The Leader and the Individual in the Younger Generation," can be found in Dietrich Bonhoeffer, *No Rusty Swords: Letters, Lectures and Notes from the Collected Works*, trans. John Bowden with Pastor Bethge, ed. and with an introduction by Edwin H. Robertson (London: Collins, Fontana Library, 1970), pp. 186–200.

11. Eberhard Bethge names the four persons and discusses stages of resistance generally in *Dietrich Bonhoeffer: Man of Vision, Man of Courage,* trans. Eric Mosbacher, Peter and Betty Ross, Frank Clarke, and William Glen-Doepel, ed. Edwin Robertson (New York: Harper & Row, 1977), pp. 696–700.

12. See Bonhoeffer, *Letters and Papers from Prison*, p. 60.

13. See Eberhard Bethge, *Bonhoeffer: Exile and Martyr*, ed. and with an Essay by John W. De Gruchy (New York: Seabury Press, 1975), pp. 155–66; and John D. Godsey, "Theologian, Christian, Contemporary," Review of *Dietrich Bonhoeffer* by Eberhard Bethge. *Interpretation* 25 (April 1971): 208–11.

14. See Dietrich Bonhoeffer, *The Communion of Saints: A Dogmatic Inquiry into the Sociology of the Church*, trans. R. Gregor Smith, foreword by Eberhard Bethge (New York: Harper & Row, 1963); and *Act and Being*, trans. Bernard Noble, introduction by Ernst Wolf (New York: Harper & Row, 1961).

15. Dietrich Bonhoeffer, *Ethics*, trans. Neville Horton Smith, ed. Eberhard Bethge (New York: Macmillan, 1965).

16. Bonhoeffer, *The Cost of Discipleship*, p. 99.

17. Bethge, *Dietrich Bonhoeffer*, p. 155, quotes this letter.

18. Marshall Berman, *The Politics of Authenticity: Radical Individualism and the Emergence of Modern Society* (New York: Atheneum, 1970), p. xix.

19. Friedrich Nietzsche, *The Will to Power*, trans. Walter Kaufmann and R. J. Hillingdale, ed., and with a commentary by Walter Kaufmann (New York: Vintage, 1968), pp. 3–4.

20. See Henry M. Pachter, "The Legend of the 20th of July, 1944," *Social Research* 29 (Spring, 1962): 109–15; George K. Romoser, "The

Politics of Uncertainty: The German Resistance Movement," *Social Research* 31 (Spring, 1964): 73–93; and Hans Rothfels, "The German Resistance Movement," *Social Research* 29 (Winter, 1962): 481–84.

21. Bonhoeffer, *Letters and Papers from Prison*, pp. 314 and 3.

22. Ernst Troeltsch, *The Social Teaching of the Christian Churches*, vol. 2, trans. Olive Wyon, with an introduction by H. Richard Niebuhr (Chicago: University of Chicago Press, 1976), p. 1013.

23. See Lucien Goldmann, *The Hidden God: A Study of Tragic Vision in the "Pensées" of Pascal and the Tragedies of Racine*, trans. Philip Thody, International Library of Philosophy and Scientific Method, ed. Ted Honderich (London: Routledge & Kegan Paul, 1964); and Max Weber, *The Protestant Ethic and the Spirit of Capitalism*, trans. Talcott Parsons, foreword by R. H. Tawney (New York: Scribner, 1958). For a good comparison of these two studies, see Terry Lovell, "Weber, Goldmann and the Sociology of Beliefs," *Archives of European Sociology* 14 (1973): 304–23.

24. Goldmann, *The Hidden God*, p. 20.

25. See, for example, Geffrey B. Kelly's review essay, "Marxist Interpretations of Bonhoeffer," *Dialog* 10 (Summer 1971): 207–20.

26. Bethge, *Dietrich Bonhoeffer*.

27. Godsey, "Theologian, Christian, Contemporary," p. 211.

28. Bethge, *Dietrich Bonhoeffer*, pp. 368–79.

29. Bethge, *Bonhoeffer: Exile and Martyr,* p. 155.

30. The major psychological interpretations of Bonhoeffer include M. F. M. van den Berk, *Bonhoeffer, boeiend en geboeid. De theologie van Dietrich Bonhoeffer in het licht van zijn persoonlijkheid* (Meppel, The Netherlands: Boom, 1974); Thomas I. Day, "Conviviality and Common Sense: The Meaning of Christian Community for Dietrich Bonhoeffer," Ph.D. dissertation, Union Theological Seminary, 1975; Thomas I. Day, *Dietrich Bonhoeffer on Christian Community and Common Sense*, Toronto Studies in Theology, vol. 11, Bonhoeffer Series, Number 2, ed. Geffrey B. Kelly (New York: The Edwin Mellen Press, 1982); Clifford J. Green, "Bonhoeffer in the Context of Erikson's Luther Study," in *Psychohistory and Religion: The Case of "Young Man Luther,"* pp. 162–96, ed. Roger A. Johnson (Philadelphia: The Fortress Press, 1977); Christian Gremmels and Hans Pfeifer, *Theologie und Biographie, Zum Beispiel Dietrich Bonhoeffer* (Munich: Chr. Kaiser, 1983); Robin W. Lovin and Jonathan P. Gosser, "Dietrich Bonhoeffer: Witness in an Ambiguous World," in *Trajectories in Faith: Five Life Stories*, pp. 147–84, ed. James W. Fowler and Robin W. Lovin with Katherine Ann Herzog, Brian Mahan, Linell Cady, and Jonathan P. Gosser (Nashville: Abingdon, 1980).

31. See, for example, Christopher Lasch, *The Culture of Narcissism: American Life in an Age of Diminishing Expectations* (New York: W. W. Norton; 1979).

32. See, for example, Marvin L. Gross, *The Psychological Society* (New York: Random House, 1978).

33. See, for example, Paul C. Vitz, *Psychology as Religion: The Cult of Self Worship* (Grand Rapids, Mi.: William B. Eerdmans; 1977).

34. Green, "Bonhoeffer in the Context of Erikson's Luther Study."

35. T. W. Adorno, Else Frenkel-Brunswik, Daniel J. Levinson, and R. Nevitt Sanford, *The Authoritarian Personality*, Studies in Prejudice, ed. Max Horkheimer and Samuel Flowerman (New York: W. W. Norton, 1969); Erich Fromm, *Escape from Freedom* (New York: Avon, 1969); David Kantor and William Lehr, *Inside the Family: Toward a Theory of Family Process* (New York: Harper & Row, 1976); and Kurt Lewin, R. Lippitt, and R. K. White, "Patterns of Aggressive Behavior in Experimentally Created 'Social Climates,'" *Journal of Social Psychology* 10 (1939): 271–99. See also Max Horkheimer, "Authority and the Family," in *Critical Theory: Selected Essays*, pp. 47–128, trans. Matthew J. O'Connell et al. (New York: Seabury Press, 1972).

36. Later writings of both Erich Fromm and Max Horkheimer suggest their changing views on the subject. See Fromm's *The Anatomy of Human Destructiveness* (New York: Holt, Rinehart and Winston, 1973) and Horkheimer's "Authoritarianism and the Family Today," in *The Family: Its Function and Destiny*, revised ed., pp. 391–98, ed. Ruth Nanda Anshen (New York: Harper & Row, 1959).

37. See Peter Lowenberg, "The Psychohistorical Origins of the Nazi Youth Cohort," *American Historical Review* 76 (December, 1971): 1457–1502.

38. I refer here to the dissertation version of Thomas I. Day's study "Conviviality and Common Sense: The Meaning of Christian Community for Dietrich Bonhoeffer." Precisely because the dissertation version of this study is so flagrant in its critique of the authoritarianism of the Bonhoeffer family, I consider this version a more illustrative example of the kind of orientation herein described (and criticized), and therefore I cite this unpublished study rather than the published version at various junctures in the argument. However, this preference should not be construed as ignorance of the altered tone of Day's book or as a suggestion that Day did not improve his interpretation.

39. The clearest statement of this theoretical orientation can be found in Ivan Boszormenyi-Nagy and Geraldine M. Spark, *Invisible Loyalties: Reciprocity in Intergenerational Family Therapy* (New York: Harper & Row, 1973). However, it should be mentioned that it was only after I had arrived at the essence of my interpretation that I discovered this text, which concisely outlined the theoretical orientation that I had been largely

developing myself. Therefore, it would be misleading for me to suggest too much theoretical allegiance to this perspective. Specifically, although my own thinking was influenced by psychoanalysis, as was the authors', I was surprised at their crediting the existentialist philosophy of Martin Buber as their second strand of intellectual influence. In my case, I was thinking largely along Durkheimian lines, trying to cull from the Durkheimian tradition of the sociology of knowledge a social psychology of knowledge that could be applied to family life. My attention was focused on the ideas of social (and family) solidarity as being a moral quality, reciprocity and exchange as the mechanism of morality, and vengeance as the primary instrument of justice. Thus it happened that the book by Boszormenyi-Nagy and Spark met me as a discovery of the sort where one finds a concise exposition of ideas that were more diffuse prior to finding it.

40. The study by Lovin and Gosser, "Dietrich Bonhoeffer: Witness in an Ambiguous World," presents a familial interpretation virtually identical to the one developed in this book. Because I discovered this study only after the present one was completed, the similarities between our interpretations suggest a certain "reliability" in the procedures. However, the Lovin and Gosser piece does not develop the interpretation as far as the present study does, specifically by linking Bonhoeffer's psychological development with the ethic of discipleship as such.

41. See Peter Berger's discussion of Bonhoeffer's sociology, "Sociology and Ecclesiology," in *The Place of Bonhoeffer: Problems and Possibilities in His Thought*, pp. 53–80, ed. Martin E. Marty (New York: Association Press, 1962). Interesting also is that Bonhoeffer fails to include Karl Marx as a sociologist whose ideas are worth reckoning with.

42. Cited in John Godsey, *The Theology of Dietrich Bonhoeffer* (Philadelphia: Westminster Press, 1960), p. 21.

43. Dietrich Bonhoeffer, *Life Together*, trans. and with an introduction by John W. Doberstein (New York: Harper & Row, 1954), p. 23.

44. This is the general tone of Bethge's interpretation, and the idea of solidarity with humanity is developed in his essay, "Modern Martyrdom," in *Bonhoeffer: Exile and Martyr*, pp. 155–66.

45. Quoted in Bethge, *Dietrich Bonhoeffer*.

46. Bonhoeffer, *The Cost of Discipleship*, p. 45.

47. Ibid., p. 47.

48. Again, Bethge's *Dietrich Bonhoeffer* details the development of the various ideas of discipleship, including the idea of costly grace.

49. van den Berk, *Bonhoeffer, boeiend en geboeid*.

50. Bonhoeffer, *The Cost of Discipleship*, p. 47.

51. Ibid., p. 45.

52. Ibid., p. 69; italics in original.

53. Bonhoeffer, *Letters and Papers from Prison*, p. 369.

CHAPTER II

1. Bonhoeffer, *The Communion of Saints*, p. 182.
2. Day, "Conviviality and Common Sense," p. 39.
3. Bethge, *Dietrich Bonhoeffer*, p. 4.
4. Mary Bosanquet, *The Life and Death of Dietrich Bonhoeffer*, foreword by Sabine Leibholz-Bonhoeffer (New York: Harper & Row, 1968).
5. Day, "Conviviality and Common Sense."
6. Eberhard Bethge, *Costly Grace: An Illustrated Introduction to Dietrich Bonhoeffer*, trans. Rosaleen Ockenden (San Francisco: Harper & Row, 1979), p. 21.
7. Sabine Leibholz-Bonhoeffer, *The Bonhoeffers: Portrait of a Family*, foreword by Lord Longford, preface by Eberhard Bethge (New York: St. Martin's Press, 1971), p. 11.
8. Quoted in Ibid.
9. Franz Hildebrandt, "An Oasis of Freedom," in *I Knew Dietrich Bonhoeffer*, pp. 38–40, ed. Wolf-Dieter Zimmermann and Ronald Gregor Smith, trans. Käthe Gregor Smith (New York: Harper & Row, 1966), p. 38.
10. Leibholz-Bonhoeffer, *The Bonhoeffers*.
11. Ibid., p. 32.
12. Ibid., p. 19.
13. Ibid., p. 16.
14. Bonhoeffer, *No Rusty Swords*, pp. 186–200.
15. Bonhoeffer, *Letters and Papers from Prison*, p. 421.
16. Emmi Bonhoeffer, "Professors' Children as Neighbors," in *I Knew Dietrich Bonhoeffer*, pp. 34–37.
17. Paul Lehmann, "Paradox of Discipleship," in *I Knew Dietrich Bonhoeffer*, pp. 41–45.
18. André Dumas, *Dietrich Bonhoeffer: Theologian of Reality*, trans. and with an introduction by Robert McAfee Brown (New York: Macmillan, 1971), p. 1.
19. Karl Barth, *The Epistle to the Romans*, 6th ed., trans. Edwyn C. Hoskyns (New York: Oxford University Press, 1968).
20. Bonhoeffer, *The Communion of Saints*, p. 33.
21. See Berger, "Sociology and Ecclesiology."
22. Dietrich Bonhoeffer, *Christ the Center*, trans. Edwin H. Robertson (New York: Harper & Row, 1978), p. 60.
23. Bonhoeffer, *Letters and Papers from Prison*, p. 282.
24. Ibid., p. 303.
25. Evidence suggests that Bonhoeffer did discuss this behavior with his fiancée, Maria von Wedemeyer. Unfortunately, however, except for a brief essay written by her and included in *Letters and Papers from Prison*

and occasional offhand remarks, little about their relationship is known. Thirty-eight letters exchanged between Bonhoeffer and her are housed at the Houghton Library at Harvard University, but they are inaccessible to the public at this time.

CHAPTER III

1. Leibholz-Bonhoeffer, *The Bonhoeffers*, p. 16.
2. Bethge, *Dietrich Bonhoeffer*, p. 4.
3. Although many works in the genre of critical theory advance this thesis, Jürgen Habermas's *Knowledge and Human Interests* (trans. Jeremy J. Shapiro [Boston: Beacon Press, 1971]) is probably the best contemporary statement of the arguments. As for Jacques Ellul, I am referring to *The Technological Society* (trans. John Wilkinson, intro. Robert K. Merton [New York: Vintage, 1964]). For Paul Tillich's similar argument, see *Systematic Theology*, vol. 1: *Reason and Revelation, Being and God* (Chicago: University of Chicago Press, 1951), pp. 71–81. Tillich, of course, was acquainted with the early critical theorists of the "Frankfurt School" prior to his and their dismissal from academic appointments in Germany by the Nazi regime.
4. Bethge, *Dietrich Bonhoeffer*, p. 21.
5. Ibid.
6. Ibid., p. 23.
7. Bonhoeffer, *Letters and Papers from Prison*, p. 94.
8. See Zerner, "Commentary," in Dietrich Bonhoeffer, *Fiction from Prison: Gathering Up the Past*, trans. Ursula Hoffmann, ed. Renate and Eberhard Bethge with Clifford Green (in the English ed.), with a Commentary by Ruth Zerner (Philadelphia: Fortress Press, 1981).
9. Clifford Green, "Introduction to the English Edition," in *Fiction from Prison*, p. ix.
10. Bonhoeffer, *Fiction from Prison*, p. 66.
11. Ibid., n. 6, pp. 175–76.
12. Leibholz-Bonhoeffer, *The Bonhoeffers,* p. 32.
13. Ibid., p. 24.
14. Eberhard Bethge, *Costly Grace: An Illustrated Introduction to Dietrich Bonhoeffer*, trans. Rosaleen Ockenden (San Francisco: Harper & Row, 1979), p. 25.
15. Leibholz-Bonhoeffer, *The Bonhoeffers*, p. 24.
16. Bethge, *Dietrich Bonhoeffer,* p. 16.

17. See Lovin and Gosser, "Dietrich Bonhoeffer: Witness in an Ambiguous World," especially note 4, pp. 204–5.

18. Bethge, *Costly Grace,* p. 27.

19. Johannes Goebel, "When He Sat Down at the Piano," in *I Knew Dietrich Bonhoeffer,* pp. 124–25.

20. Leibholz-Bonhoeffer, "Childhood and Home," in *I Knew Dietrich Bonhoeffer,* p. 23.

21. Quoted in Bethge, *Dietrich Bonhoeffer,* pp. 24–25.

22. Bonhoeffer, *Letters and Papers from Prison,* p. 16.

23. Bonhoeffer, *The Cost of Discipleship,* p. 100.

24. Bonhoeffer, *Letters and Papers from Prison,* p. 275.

25. Bethge, *Dietrich Bonhoeffer,* p. 39.

26. Ibid., p. 43.

27. International Bonhoeffer Society for Archive and Research, English Language Section, *Newsletter* 28 (November 1984): 3.

CHAPTER IV

1. Dietrich Bonhoeffer, *Creation and Fall: A Theological Interpretation of Genesis 1–3,* trans. John C. Fletcher (New York: Macmillan, 1959), p. 38.

2. Ibid., p. 79.

3. Bethge, *Dietrich Bonhoeffer,* pp. 25–27.

4. Erik H. Erikson, *Young Man Luther: A Study in Psychoanalysis and History* (New York: W. W. Norton, 1962), pp. 156–57.

5. Bethge, *Dietrich Bonhoeffer,* p. 23.

6. Bonhoeffer, *No Rusty Swords,* p. 116.

7. Ibid., p. 114.

8. Ibid., p. 200.

9. Ibid., p. 230.

10. Ibid., p. 235.

11. Dietrich Bonhoeffer, *The Way to Freedom: Letters, Lectures and Notes 1935–1939 from the Collected Works,* trans. Edwin H. Robertson and John Bowden, ed. and with an introduction by Edwin H. Robertson (New York: Harper & Row, 1973), p. 116.

12. Ibid., p. 119.

13. Ibid., p. 116.

14. Ibid., p. 119.

15. Ibid., p. 121.

16. International Bonhoeffer Society for Archive and Research, English Language Section, *Newsletter* 22 (June, 1982).

17. Bonhoeffer, *Letters and Papers from Prison*, pp. 280, 286, 328f.

18. Hellmut Traub, "Two Recollections," in *I Knew Dietrich Bonhoeffer*, pp. 156–61.

19. Bonhoeffer, *The Way to Freedom*, p. 227.

20. Ibid., p. 246.

21. Ibid., p. 233.

22. Ibid.

Chapter V

1. For a good discussion of the conflict between Narcissus and community in western civilization, see Paul Zweig, *The Heresy of Self-Love: A Study of Subversive Individualism* (Princeton, NJ: Princeton University Press, 1980).

2. Quoted in Mary Jo Bane, *Here to Stay: American Families in the Twentieth Century* (New York: Basic Books, 1976), p. 71.

3. Aristotle, 1252^a 30–31.

4. The work that inaugurated the contemporary study of psychohistory.

5. By Clifford Green.

6. Bonhoeffer, *Letters and Papers from Prison*, p. 3.

7. Erik H. Erikson, *Gandhi's Truth: On the Origins of Militant Non-Violence* (New York: W. W. Norton, 1969), p. 222.

8. See Margaret R. Miles, "Infancy, Parenting, and Nourishment in Augustine's *Confessions,*" *Journal of the American Academy of Religion* 50 (September 1982): 354.

9. Bonhoeffer, *Letters and Papers from Prison*, p. 314.

10. Ibid., p. 245.

11. Erikson, *Gandhi's Truth*, p. 128.

12. Bonhoeffer, *The Cost of Discipleship*, p. 62.

13. Bonhoeffer, *Ethics*, p. 121.

14. Ibid., p. 250.

15. Bonhoeffer, *No Rusty Swords*, p. 199.

16. Bonhoeffer, *Ethics*, pp. 120–87, 332–53.

17. Zerner, "Dietrich Bonhoeffer's Prison Fiction: A Commentary," in *Fiction from Prison*, p. 159.

18. Bonhoeffer, *Fiction from Prison*, p. 87.

19. Hannah Arendt, *Eichmann in Jerusalem: A Report on the Banality of Evil* (New York: Penguin Books, 1977), p. 33.

20. Bonhoeffer, *Ethics*, p. 98.

21. Ibid., p. 354.

22. Ibid., pp. 272–73.

23. Ibid., p. 102.

24. Ibid., p. 150.

25. Weber, *The Protestant Ethic*, p. 182.

26. Ibid.

27. Bonhoeffer, *Letters and Papers from Prison*, p. 279.

28. Unfortunately, I have mislaid the English translation of this quotation. However, the German may be found in Dietrich Bonhoeffer, *Gesammelte Schriften,* Zweiter Band, ed. Eberhard Bethge (Munich: Chr. Kaiser, 1965), p. 553.

29. Bonhoeffer, *Letters and Papers from Prison*, p. 176.

30. Ibid., p. 286.

31. Ibid., p. 360.

Bibliography

Note on Sources

The primary sources used in this study include Bonhoeffer's published and posthumously published works, as well as his diaries, lectures, notes, sermons, and the like. For the most part, this latter array of sources is compiled in the six volumes of *Gesammelte Schriften,* edited by Bonhoeffer's student and friend Eberhard Bethge. In general, when citing these sources in the text I have referred to their English translations. Bonhoeffer scholars often object to this reliance upon English-language sources on the grounds both that reservations have been raised about the quality of some of the translations and that a sizeable portion of primary material remains untranslated. However, these problems can be remedied somewhat by a careful consideration of the points made in John D. Godsey's article, "Reading Bonhoeffer in English Translation: Some Difficulties," by consulting the German originals at crucial junctures of the interpretation, and by engaging scholars thoroughly acquainted with the German materials to clarify obscure cross-cultural points. All of these partial remedies have been effected for the present study. Of special note for a psychological interpretation is the recent appearance of Ursula Hoffmann's English translation of Bonhoeffer's *Fiction from Prison: Gathering Up the Past,* edited by Renate and Eberhard Bethge with Clifford Green. This work is rich in psychological information, with its some two hundred and fifty footnotes, a commentary, and introductions by Bonhoeffer scholars and intimates.

In a psychological interpretation of Bonhoeffer, certain secondary sources might also be considered primary ones. These include, especially, the three books by Bethge, the book by Bonhoeffer's twin sister on their family, the collection of personal recollections in *I Knew Dietrich Bonhoeffer,* and various essays by intimates that appear in different places (often as forewords to Bonhoeffer's books). Thus, for example, although Bethge's works are of the highest scholarly standards, they are cited throughout this study more as a source of primary data than as an interpretive perspective with which I interact. For that reason, the frequency with which Bethge is cited in the book should not be construed as evidence that I consider him to be my main interlocutor—to the neglect of dialogue with other responsible interpretations—but should be accounted for simply on the ground that Bethge is one of a handful of people who possess and have published authoritative facts about Bonhoeffer's life and thought.

On the matter of secondary sources, the reader is referred to the notes and bibliography. There are several Bonhoeffer bibliographies in German, and an English-language bibliography was compiled by Clifford J. Green in "Bonhoeffer Bibliography: English Language Sources" (*Union Seminary Quarterly Review* 31 [Summer 1976]: 227–60). This English-language bibliography is periodically updated in the *Newsletters* of the International Bonhoeffer Society for Archive and Research, English Language Section. In general, conceiving the main contribution of this study to reside in psychology and social thought rather than Bonhoeffer scholarship narrowly understood, I have avoided lengthy debates with extant Bonhoeffer interpretations, preferring to limit my discussions to issues in my own discipline and to limit my citations of Bonhoeffer studies to those with either a direct bearing on mine or else those of a general nature. Readers interested in Bonhoeffer studies per se are advised to contact the International Bonhoeffer Society for Archive and Research, the English-language archives being located at Union Theological Seminary in New York.

I. Works by Dietrich Bonhoeffer

Act and Being. Translated by Bernard Noble. Introduction by Ernst Wolf. New York: Harper & Row, 1961.

Christ the Center. Translated by Edwin H. Robertson. New York: Harper & Row, 1978.

The Communion of Saints: A Dogmatic Inquiry into the Sociology of the Church. Translated by R. Gregor Smith. Foreword by Eberhard Bethge. New York: Harper & Row, 1963.

The Cost of Discipleship. Revised Edition. Translated by R. H. Fuller. Foreword by Bishop G. K. A. Bell. Memoir by G. Leibholz. New York: Macmillan, 1963.

Creation and Fall: A Theological Interpretation of Genesis 1–3. Translated by John C. Fletcher. Published together with *Temptation.* Translated by Kathleen Downham. Edited by Eberhard Bethge. New York: Macmillan, 1959.

Ethics. Translated by Neville Horton Smith. Edited by Eberhard Bethge. New York: Macmillan, 1965.

Fiction from Prison: Gathering Up the Past. Translated by Ursula Hoffmann. Edited by Renate and Eberhard Bethge with Clifford Green (in the English Edition). Commentary by Ruth Zerner. Philadelphia: Fortress Press, 1981.

Gesammelte Schriften. 6 vols. Edited by Eberhard Bethge. Munch: Chr. Kaiser Verlag, 1956–1974.

Letters and Papers from Prison. Enlarged Edition. Translated by Reginald Fuller, Frank Clarke and others. Edited by Eberhard Bethge. New York: Macmillan, 1972.

Life Together. Translated and with an Introduction by John W. Doberstein. New York: Harper & Row, 1954.

No Rusty Swords: Letters, Lectures and Notes 1928–1936 from the Collected Works. Translated by John Bowden with Pastor Bethge. Edited and with an Introduction by Edwin H. Robertson. London: Collins, The Fontana Library, 1970.

True Patriotism: Letters, Lectures and Notes 1939–1945 from the Collected Works. Translated by Edwin H. Robertson and John Bowden. Edited and with an Introduction by Edwin H. Robertson. New York: Harper & Row, 1973.

The Way to Freedom: Letters, Lectures and Notes 1935–1939 from the Collected Works. Translated by Edwin H. Robertson and John Bowden. Edited and with an Introduction by Edwin H. Robertson. New York: Harper & Row, 1966.

II. Works about Bonhoeffer

Abercrombie, Clarence L. "Barth and Bonhoeffer: Resistance to the Unjust State." *Religion in Life* 42 (Autumn 1973): 344–60.

Bethge, Eberhard. *Bonhoeffer: Exile and Martyr.* Edited and with an Essay by John W. de Gruchy. New York: Seabury Press, 1975.

———. *Costly Grace: An Illustrated Introduction to Dietrich Bonhoeffer.* Translated by Rosaleen Ockenden. New York: Harper & Row, 1979.

———. *Dietrich Bonhoeffer: Man of Vision, Man of Courage.* Translated by Eric Mosbacher, Peter and Betty Ross, Frank Clarke, and

William Glen-Doepel, under the editorship of Edwin H. Robertson. New York: Harper & Row, 1970.

Bosanquet, Mary. *The Life and Death of Dietrich Bonhoeffer.* Foreword
by Sabine Leibholz-Bonhoeffer. New York: Harper & Row, 1968.

Day, Thomas I. "Conviviality and Common Sense: The Meaning of Christian Community for Dietrich Bonhoeffer." Ph.D. dissertation,
Union Theological Seminary, 1975.

————. *Dietrich Bonhoeffer on Christian Community and Common Sense.*
Toronto Studies in Theology, vol. 11. Bonhoeffer Series, Num-
ber 2. Edited by Geffrey B. Kelly. New York: The Edwin Mellen
Press, 1982.

Dumas, André. *Dietrich Bonhoeffer: Theologian of Reality.* Translated by
Robert McAfee Brown. New York: Macmillan, 1971.

Godsey, John D. "Reading Bonhoeffer in English Translation: Some Difficulties." *Union Seminary Quarterly Review* 23 (Fall 1967): 79–
90.

————. "Theologian, Christian, Contemporary." Review of *Dietrich Bonhoeffer,* by Eberhard Bethge. *Interpretation* 25 (April 1971):
208–11.

Godsey, John D., and Kelly, Geffrey B., eds., *Ethical Responsibility: Bonhoeffer's Legacy to the Churches.* Toronto Studies in Theology,
vol. 6. New York: The Edwin Mellen Press, 1981.

Green, Clifford J. "Bonhoeffer in the Context of Erikson's Luther Study."
In *Psychohistory and Religion: The Case of Young Man Luther,*
pp. 162–96. Edited by Roger A. Johnson. Philadelphia: Fortress
Press, 1977.

————. *The Sociality of Christ and Humanity: Dietrich Bonhoeffer's Early
Theology, 1927–1933.* American Academy of Religion Disser-
tation Series. Edited by H. Ganse Little, Jr. Missoula: Scholars
Press, 1972.

Gremmels, Christian, and Pfeifer, Hans. *Theologie und Biographie, Zum
Beispiel Dietrich Bonhoeffer.* Munich: Chr. Kaiser Verlag, 1983.

Holbrook, Clyde A. "The Problem of Authority in Christian Ethics." *Journal of the American Academy of Religion* 37 (March 1969): 26–
48.

Hopper, David H. *A Dissent on Bonhoeffer.* Philadelphia: Westminster
Press, 1975.

Kelly, Geffrey B. "Marxist Interpretations of Bonhoeffer." *Dialog* 10 (Summer 1971): 207–20.

Leibholz-Bonhoeffer, Sabine. *The Bonhoeffers: Portrait of a Family.* Fore-
    word by Lord Longford. Preface by Eberhard Bethge. New York:
    St. Martin's Press, 1971.
Lovin, Robin W., and Gosser, Jonathan P. "Dietrich Bonhoeffer: Witness
    in an Ambiguous World." In *Trajectories in Faith: Five Life Sto-
    ries,* pp. 147–84. Edited by James W. Fowler and Robin W. Lovin
    with Katherine Ann Herzog, Brian Mahan, Linell Cady, and
    Jonathan P. Gosser. Nashville: Abingdon, 1980.
Marty, Martin E., ed. *The Place of Bonhoeffer: Problems and Possibilities
    in His Thought.* New York: Association Press, 1962.
Ott, Heinrich. *Reality and Faith: The Theological Legacy of Dietrich Bon-
    hoeffer.* Translated by Alex A. Morrison. Philadelphia: Fortress
    Press, 1972.
Palmer, Russell W. "Demythologizing and Non-Religious Interpretation:
    A Comparison of Bultman and Bonhoeffer." *Iliff Review* 31 (Spring
    1974): 3–15.
Peters, Tiemo Rainer, *Die Präsenz des Politischen in der Theologie Die-
    trich Bonhoeffers.* Grünewald: Chr. Kaiser Verlag, 1976.
Ruether, Rosemary. "A Query to Daniel Sullivan: Bonhoeffer on Sexuality."
    Continuum 4 (Autumn 1966): 457–60.
van den Berk, M. F. M. *Bonhoeffer, boeiend en geboeid. De theologie van
    Dietrich Bonhoeffer in het licht van zijn persoonlijkheid.* Mep-
    pel, The Netherlands: Boom Publishers, 1974.
Zimmerman, Wolf-Dieter, and Smith, Ronald Gregor, eds. *I Knew Dietrich
    Bonhoeffer.* Translated by Käthe Gregor Smith. New York: Har-
    per & Row, 1966.

III. Other Works Consulted

Adorno, T. W.; Frenkel-Brunswik, Else; Levinson, Daniel J.; and Sanford,
    R. Nevitt. *The Authoritarian Personality.* Studies in Prejudice.
    Edited by Max Horkheimer and Samuel Flowerman. New York:
    W. W. Norton, 1969.
Arendt, Hannah. *Between Past and Future: Eight Exercises in Political
    Thought.* New York: Penguin Books, 1977.

————. *Eichmann in Jerusalem: A Report on the Banality of Evil.* New York: Penguin Books, 1977.

————. *The Origins of Totalitarianism.* New York: Harcourt Brace Jovanovich, 1973.

Boszormenyi-Nagy, Ivan, and Spark, Geraldine M. *Invisible Loyalties: Reciprocity in Intergenerational Family Therapy.* New York: Harper & Row, 1973.

Christie, Richard, and Jahoda, Marie, eds. *Studies in the Scope and Method of "The Authoritarian Personality."* Glencoe, IL: Free Press, 1954.

Erikson, Erik H. *Gandhi's Truth: On the Origins of Militant Nonviolence.* New York: W. W. Norton, 1969.

————. *Life History and the Historical Moment.* New York: W. W. Norton, 1975.

————. *Young Man Luther: A Study in Psychoanalysis and History.* New York: W. W. Norton, 1962.

Fromm, Erich. *Escape from Freedom.* New York: Avon, 1969.

Greenstein, Fred I. "Personality and Political Socialization: The Theories of Authoritarian and Democratic Character." *The Annals of the American Academy of Political and Social Science* 361 (1965): 81–93.

Goldmann, Lucien. *The Hidden God: A Study of Tragic Vision in the "Pensées" of Pascal and the Tragedies of Racine.* Translated by Philip Thody. London: Routledge & Kegan Paul, 1964.

Helmreich, Ernst Christian. *The German Churches Under Hitler: Background, Struggle and Epilogue.* Detroit: Wayne State University Press, 1979.

Horkheimer, Max. "Authoritarianism and the Family." In *The Family: Its Function and Destiny,* revised, pp. 381–98. Edited by Ruth Nanda Anshen. New York: Harper & Row, 1959.

————. "Authority and the Family." In *Critical Theory: Selected Essays,* pp. 47–128. Translated by Matthew J. O'Connell and others. New York: Seabury Press, 1972.

Kantor, David, and Lehr, William. *Inside the Family: Toward a Theory of Family Process.* New York: Harper & Row, 1976.

Lowenberg, Peter. "The Psychohistorical Origins of the Nazi Youth Cohort." *American Historical Review* 76 (December 1971): 1457–1502.

Maslow, Abraham H. "The Authoritarian Character Structure." *Journal of Social Psychology* 18 (1943): 401–11.

Nelson, F. Burton. "The Holocaust and the American Future." *Radix* 12 (January/February 1981): 5–9.

Pachter, Henry M. "The Legend of the 20th of July, 1944." *Social Research* 29 (Spring 1962): 109–15.

Robertson, Roland, and Holzner, Burhart, eds. *Identity and Authority: Exploration in the Theory of Society.* New York: St. Martin's Press, 1979.

Romoser, George K. "The Politics of Uncertainty: The German Resistance Movement." *Social Research* 31 (Spring 1964): 73–93.

Rothfels, Hans. "The German Resistance Movement." *Social Research* 29 (Winter 1962): 481–84.

Selzner, Michael. "Psychohistorical Approaches to the Study of Nazism." *Journal of Psychohistory* 4 (Fall 1976): 215–24.

Sennett, Richard. *Authority.* New York: Vintage Books, 1980.

Weber, Max. *The Protestant Ethic and the Spirit of Capitalism.* Translated by Talcott Parsons. Foreword by R. H. Tawney. New York: Charles Scribner's Sons, 1958.

Index